MEN
OF
DESTINY

LENIN, 1918

LENIN

James Maxton

Distributed by
HERON BOOKS

Published by arrangement with
Peter Davies Ltd.

I

THE year 1932 finds a world sore perplexed with its economic worries. Powerful nations with a long history of industrial and social progress feel their foundations unstable. Men fear a crash that might wipe out in months the progress of centuries. Knowledge, skill, scientific devices, productive capacity are at a higher point than ever before, but some basic defects in the method of utilising these factors at this juncture in history prevent them from rendering their fruits to mankind and create a position full of menace. Millions of competent workers stand idle in the streets of New York, Berlin, London, Sydney, and the plant, machinery and material for the handling of which they possess the necessary skill lie unused and deteriorating. From early times man has dreamt of an age of plenty. Prophets have foretold the coming of a Utopia where work would be light and the material needs of life would be satisfied with ease and abundance for all. When for the first time in history the conditions for the realisation of the dream seem nearly in their grasp, instead of confidence and hope, fear fills the minds of men.

In the midst of this doubting, fearing world stands Russia, until a dozen years ago despised among nations for her backwardness, her lack of initiative, her mediaeval sluggishness—the outstanding example to the world of a brutal tyranny standing over an ignorant, superstitious, terrorised populace. To-day, while the rest of the world sends out cries of despair and discusses the possibility of bankruptcy, from Russia there come confident reports of great industrial and agricultural developments, the erection of factories, electrical plants, the organisation of huge farms with all the finest mechanical aids, the rapid spread of literacy among a previously illiterate population, and the development of technical skill among an unskilled people.

Whence came the impetus ? why this confidence ? who has propounded the plan ? What good fairy waved the magic wand that roused this sleeping giant from his slumbers, and breathed vigorous confident life into his veins, when elsewhere nations active, prominent, with records of achievement, fainted and almost fell by the way ?

6

The scientific answer to these questions would produce a long list of antecedent causes recorded in the history of the Russian people. It would contain a black history of degrading poverty, a sordid struggle with soil and forest for a bare subsistence. It would tell of Czars, of great landlords holding power of life and death over their serfs, of the lash of the knout, of dark gloomy fortress prisons, of the Siberian snows. It would tell of spasmodic outbursts against tyranny, of the attempts to remove despots by deeds of violence, of heroic figures and noble writers protesting ineffectively against the lot of the people.

But standing out above all the scientific reasons, economic and historical, above the poets and writers, dwarfing everything and every one, is the man Lenin, interpreter of Russia, liberator of Russia, inspirer and initiator of the New Russia. To large masses of common people the world over he stands, not merely as the Russian liberator and the founder of a New Russia, but as the pioneer of a new world order which, having resolved the economic difficulties that confront the nations today, will usher in the age of plenty and give to all mankind that free and abundant life which has till now been only a dream. Whether the future prove this fact or phantasy, whether the personality of Lenin fails to project itself beyond the bounds of Russia or whether the present Russian experiments disappoint the high hopes placed in them by the mass of the Russian people, the figure of Lenin will still remain an outstanding one among historic persons. It is important, therefore, that a knowledge of this man and his life should be widespread among those who tend to deify him, among those who would classify him as some monster, and also among those who would prefer to dismiss him, his work and his thought as of no permanent significance.

He appeared in the middle of the stage in the year 1917 out of the smoke and thunder of the great European war, almost unheralded, certainly unwelcomed by the war mind that dominated world thought and world activity at that time. The great slaughter had then continued for more than three years. The glamour of it had gone. The hopes of a glittering victory for one side or the other had faded. Men began to desire the end, but none was willing to give in ; no one was ready for peace without victory, and there was a feeling that the two opposing forces, facing each other entrenched in long lines of holes in the ground, might continue for years in a position of stalemate, with the armies gradually destroying each other and the civilian populations moving towards complete starvation.

In such circumstances it was natural that the Allied nations should consider their own and their Allies' resources of men and material and find fault with each others' contribution to the common task. Russia, both as regards territory and population, was much the largest of the nations involved, but a feeling grew up that she was not producing results in proportion to her strength. Whether or not the Allied nations did propaganda on this theme in Russia itself is not clear, but war propaganda generally was conducted by subtle and devious means in all the Allied countries, and it was always difficult to trace accurately its source. Certainly there grew up in Russia itself the view that the war effort was not being directed with real energy, and the Russian royal family came under the suspicion of having pro-German sympathies. The more prosperous classes, with strong views about the energetic prosecution of the war, were primarily responsible for the propaganda against Czar Nicholas, but war weariness among the soldiers and privation among the civilian population gave it real strength and meaning, and on 2nd March 1917 the Czar abdicated. The Provisional Government then set up was hailed among the Allies with great satisfaction. It stood for the more energetic prosecution of the war. It had some appearance of democratic authority of the type known in France, England and Belgium, and its outlook was similar. It failed to establish itself. It was one thing to start a revolutionary movement, an entirely different thing to halt it. The people wanted something other than the energetic prosecution of the war, and the first Provisional Government of a Liberal complexion had speedily to give place to a Government of a Social-reformist type under the leadership of Kerensky, which seemed to offer some hope of dealing at least with the privations of the people, and which at least, if not yet ready for the abrupt cessation of hostilities, would not stand for the policy of the 'last shilling and the last man.'

This Kerensky Government also failed to establish itself. The Russian people wanted something more than it appeared ready and able to give. The soldiers were war weary, the people were hungry. They were impatient of questions regarding the machinery of government, were not deeply concerned about parliamentary institutions planned on Western models, were not impressed by intricate diplomatic negotiations with other powers. They wanted to get out of the war, and wanted to get out quickly. They wanted bread, and wanted it immediately.

In such circumstances Lenin presented himself in the centre of the world historical stage and filled the rôle that the masses of Russia were clamouring for. It is not an over-statement to say that he was an unknown person in the public life of the world until October 1917. From that date his personality penetrates the most remote corners of the globe. This fact must remain as one of the wonders of history. Here was no great soldier who had won fame by deeds of gallantry or military genius on the tented field. He had never buckled on a sword or shouldered a gun— except a sporting gun when he sallied forth to shoot wild-duck. He was no world statesman who had won fame in parliament or council by forensic skill or political subtlety. He was no literary genius whose writings, reaching the hearts of a whole nation, had made his name a household word. He had not even established a reputation as a great lawyer successfully championing in the courts oppressed and suffering individuals. He was a plain man who had appeared out of obscurity to meet a need felt keenly by 150 millions of people, in the armies of Russia, in the factories and streets of Moscow and Petrograd, and in the thousands of villages scattered over the vast plains of Russia.

On the surface it seemed as if the need for the man had arisen by a series of accidental and unconnected happenings and that the man had just as accidentally arrived to meet the need. The facts beneath the outward appearance were otherwise. Lenin had anticipated the arrival of such a moment. As the astronomer might work out in his observatory the arrival of a particular star in the heavens, so had Lenin visualised the nature of the situation to be dealt with. He had prepared himself to meet its problems when they arose on principles, by methods and devices thought out in advance and in the abstract, but capable of adaptation and elasticity to suit the situation in its concrete form. He had enlisted and trained a band of helpers competent to assist him in the huge task, and had inspired them with a great confidence in himself as a man in whose hands they could place their destinies, and to whose orders they could safely subordinate themselves with the assurance that under his orders their efforts would be directed towards ends that were their own.

The situation that he had anticipated in his theorising arrived. He placed himself in the middle of it. His band of assistants and co-workers rallied round him ; the masses of the Russian people responded as he had believed that they would respond ; the Revolution was accomplished.

II

LENIN was born on the 10th April 1870, at Simbirsk on the Volga. The name Lenin he adopted in his early manhood when he became actively engaged in political life. His own name was Vladimir Ilyich Ul'yanov. His parents were people of some social standing in those days, his father holding a responsible position in the educational service of the Province of Simbirsk, while his mother was of the landowning class, her family owning a small estate in the Province of Kazan. Of his father's political and social outlook no record appears in any of the presently available sources of information, and it is probable that he found it—in the then prevailing conditions in Russia —wiser to have no views on political matters, as indeed civil servants in most circumstances find it wiser to observe a very great reticence as to their political ideas and aspirations. It is difficult however to believe, having regard to the record of the sons and daughters, that in the parental influence in the home, either from the father or the mother, there was not some stimulus that directed the minds of the family along the revolutionary road. There were three sons and three daughters, and all, practically in the adolescent period, turned to revolutionary thought and activity.

Political feeling in Russia at this period was strong. From 1856 onwards, in the years following the Crimean war, she began to copy the capitalist models which were already well established in Britain, Germany and France. In the period round 1860 serfdom was abolished and certain steps were taken towards the establishment of local self-government. Parallel with the movement by the ruling classes to copy Western ideas, there developed among other sections in Russia the desire for fundamental social changes. Socialist theories were already well formulated in Germany, and working-class movements for social amelioration and political status were developing in Britain along the lines of Chartism, trade unionism and the Co-operative Society. France had been through stirring times. In September 1870 the French Empire fell, and a Republic was declared ; and in March of the following year the working men of Paris rose in revolution and proclaimed the Paris Commune, which was to be the initial step in the creation of a French Socialist

Commonwealth. It was a short-lived triumph, but sufficient to strike the imagination of oppressed workers in many parts of Europe. The Russian masses, mainly peasants emerging fresh from serfdom, were not soil on which this revolutionary seed could fructify, but in the minds of that minority of young Russians who had had the advantages of education such ideas readily took root.

The Ul'yanov family was swept into this current and carried along by it, the eldest son Alexandre to his doom in 1887. One of Lenin's sisters died when a young student, but the others were throughout enthusiastic workers in the revolutionary movement, and their mother always kept up her sympathetic support of and contact with them. Their father died in 1886, and was spared the mental torment that the mother must have endured almost continuously over the dangers faced and the privations suffered by her spirited offspring, who had chosen to tread a path which meant a life of constant hazard in the Russia of those days.

Vladimir received a good education of the orthodox type. He attended the High School of Simbirsk until the age of eighteen, at which school the headmaster was the father of Kerensky, whom Lenin subsequently deposed from his position as head of the Provisional Government. It is recorded that he took first place in the final examinations in his school, an achievement which sheds a remarkable light on his mind and character. Already at the age of seventeen he had become absorbed in Marxist and other revolutionary literature, and at this time was spending a large proportion of his leisure in the study of Socialist works. His whole being was aflame with interest in them, and in comparison the school subjects must have appeared trivial and their study irksome to him.

His brother Alexandre died on the scaffold in the spring of that year (1887) for participation in an attempt on the life of the Czar. His death was not merely a frightful blow to Ilyich, since there was a great community of interest between the two brothers, but it brought the whole family into public disrepute and under police ban. It was only through influential intervention on his behalf that Lenin was permitted to sit his final school examinations at all. In such circumstances to come through such a test with distinction displayed a type of mind and a power of self-mastery and concentration very striking in a youth of seventeen years. These qualities of mind stayed with him and developed throughout his life, and at the stormiest and most difficult periods he could detach himself from problems that would have overwhelmed most men and concentrate on some comparatively minor matter which required immediate attention. The certificate from his schoolmaster bore the words: 'Very gifted; consistently painstaking and regular in his attendance.'

It has been suggested in certain quarters that the death of his brother embittered him and that his subsequent life was one long struggle to have revenge upon the Czarist power that had taken from him a beloved brother. There is no evidence of him as a personally embittered man, nor is there any indication anywhere of the attempt on his part to serve purely personal ends by his activities. His reaction to the tragic event seems to have been a wholly different one. It impressed him strongly with the futility of terroristic acts by individuals against highly placed persons as a policy for achieving fundamental social changes. It made him grasp more clearly than before the view that in any social system power rests in the hands of the class that is economically strong, and that a real movement for liberation must work, not by attacks on individual tyrants, but by the organisation of the workers as a class with the definite aim of seizing economic power. To obtain the election of workers to particular political positions or to remove objectionable individuals from particular political positions by acts of terror was of no value. His personal loss, the causes that brought it about, certainly forced him to examine very closely the aims and objects desired by his brother Alexandre, and drove him to the conclusion, which influenced his whole life and thought, that these aims and objects could not be achieved by Alexandre's method, however wicked the tyrant destroyed or however heroic the revolutionist who gave his life to destroy him.

Simbirsk, a town of some 30,000 inhabitants on the banks of the Middle Volga, with summer holiday periods spent in the more rural district in Kazan where his mother's people lived, provided suitable surroundings in which the youthful Lenin could absorb almost unconsciously that knowledge of the Russian people—peasants and workers—that understanding of their unexpressed longings and desires, which was an even more important part of his intellectual equipment than the official studies of his school-days or the subsequent experiences of his University life which marked the next stage in his life.

III

FROM school in the autumn of 1887 Lenin proceeded to the University of Kazan with the intention of studying law. His residence there was probably one of the shortest University careers on record. The students at a provincial University like Kazan were at that time mainly the sons of people who were not well off, struggling to get a University education that would give them the hall-mark necessary for admission to positions of one kind and another in the public service. While the general atmosphere may not have been one of high thinking, it was certainly one of low living in the material sense. The students did their work under conditions of great privation, both as to accommodation and food, and these conditions very readily encouraged the development of seditious sentiments and movements among the student class. Such movements were largely spasmodic, their aims and objects not very clearly defined, and when finding expression were probably not of greater significance than

the disturbances created by the undergraduates
in British Universities which are usually attri-
buted in this country to the exuberant animal
spirits of youth. The University and national
authorities in Russia took a more serious view.
Such a disturbance occurred a week or two
after Lenin's arrival at Kazan. He was
marked down by the authorities as one of the
ringleaders, although freshmen of a few weeks'
standing are not generally promoted by the
undergraduate genus to such prominence. It
is probable that he was ' the dog with the bad
name ' on account of his brother's record, and
he had to pay the penalty. He was sent down
after a University career lasting barely one
month, and banished to the home of his
mother's people in the country at Kokushkino.
His banishment did not destroy his desire for
knowledge, nor for a University qualification.
He continued his law studies and made repeated efforts to secure readmission to Kazan,
or to any other University, and even to get
permission to proceed abroad. All these re-
quests were refused, but the student stuck to
his books, assiduously following the prescribed
courses with himself as his own guide and
tutor. His capacity as a student was again
demonstrated when in 1890 he was at last

permitted to sit the law examinations at St. Petersburg University as an external student. He passed his examinations successfully, and was admitted to a law degree.

Along with his law studies he had pursued the study of the Marxian philosophy and economics, to which he had been introduced when at school. This study must have presented to his mind a complete contrast to Russian Czarist jurisprudence and made much deeper and more lasting impressions on his mind ; it was a much more potent influence in forming his character and directing his future life.

Reference has already been made to the work of Marx, and it is necessary in Britain— where neither the man nor his work has ever been sufficiently well known—to give some description to convey an idea of the stature of the man and the scope of his work which had such an important influence on the development of Lenin, as indeed it had on working-class movements throughout the world.

Karl Marx was born in Germany in 1818 and died in London in 1873. His father was a lawyer of Jewish origin who had joined the Christian Church. Like Lenin, Marx went to the University to study law, first at Bonn and

afterwards at Berlin, but he carried his studies
far beyond the ordinary limits of the law student
and particularly devoted himself to the study
of history and philosophy. He came strongly
under the influence of the philosophic teaching
of Hegel. He rejected the idea of a career in
law or in the public services of Germany which
his father desired for him, and set his course to
become a lecturer in philosophy in a German
University. To that end, in 1841, he took the
degree of Doctor of Philosophy at the University of Jena. But already his outspoken and
unorthodox views on philosophy had become
sufficiently known in German Academic circles
to close that door to him. He turned to the
pen as the instrument by which he should at
one and the same time earn his bread and
propagate the ideas of freedom which already
possessed him.

The effect of the attitude of the University
of Kazan towards Lenin and of the University
of Bonn towards Marx on the future course of
world history is worth a moment's thought.
The one wished to nip in the bud the agita-
tional power and disregard for authority in a
young undergraduate ; the other endeavoured
to stifle at birth the undeveloped, new ideas in
philosophy and economics appearing in the

work of a graduate and prospective University teacher. They both failed signally, and both in their attempt and their failure gave to the world two of its most potent personalities.

In 1842 Marx became a contributor to the *Rheinische Zeitung*, a newspaper of Liberal outlook, and at the end of that year became its editor. In the two years during which he occupied that position he became a Socialist through his study of the then available French Socialist literature and his own original thought on the economic problems of his time. Applying his own philosophic mind and particularly his own adaptation of the Hegelian system to that literature and to current economic problems, he carried Socialist theory on to an entirely new plane.

He removed to Paris and there established contact for the first time with Frederic Engels, a German manufacturer who was in business in Manchester. Engels in turn had been in association with Robert Owen, who may be taken as the pioneer of the British working-class movement and is generally recognised as the founder of the Co-operative Society Movement which has grown from trivial beginnings to its present imposing dimensions. When

Engels met Marx in Paris his outlook on social problems was mainly of the Owenite stamp, but the two men formed a life partnership which resulted in the formulation of a Socialist theory with a philosophic and scientific basis and with a revolutionary method and objective. Marx was the senior partner, always devoting his whole time (for the most part spent in exile) to the production of writings propounding his Socialist theory. His literary style was much affected by philosophic and scientific terminology, not well suited for direct appeal to working-class readers to whom its teaching might be expected to appeal, and no brief and simple summary is possible.

Starting from the view that dreaming of ideal states, depicting Utopias, and planning new social systems does not bring them into existence, he dismissed summarily the work of earlier Socialists, and made the proposition that human progress on this planet proceeds, not haphazard, but according to scientific laws. It is the duty of the Socialist to discover these laws and to formulate them, so that those who desire social progress may be enabled to work in conformity with those laws. Moulding Hegel's work on thought processes, termed by him the Dialectic, to his own ends, Marx built up stage by stage a very complete theory, the important elements in which are the materialist conception of history, the theory of class struggle, the economic fact of surplus value as the factor which produces capitalist accumulation and which produces finally the insoluble contradictions inside the capitalist system.

There has been a myriad of critics who have turned his work inside out, challenged its claim to be either scientific or philosophic, have taken it to pieces and asserted that those parts which had validity were not the original work of Karl Marx. This experience, however, has not been confined to Marx and his work, but has been the lot of every philosopher and scientist from Socrates to Einstein. The fact remains written in world history, that whatever errors there may be in the theories of Marx, whatever adjustments may become necessary in the light of future knowledge, his hypotheses have provided workers in the realm of sociology and politics with illuminating conceptions which have guided and inspired them in their practical work. Amongst those who received their stimulus from this source Lenin takes the foremost place. He himself summarised the place of Marx in the realm of thought in the following terms : ' Marx continued and completed, genius fashion, the three main spiritual tendencies of the nineteenth century, represented by the three foremost countries of humanity : classical German philosophy, classical English political economy and French Socialism.' [1]

While Marxism still struggled painfully for acceptance among the scientists and philosophers of a social system whose end it prophesied, an end which it proposed to hasten, it came to the masses with the force of a religion. It was a gospel of salvation, the poor heard it gladly ; not for them hairsplitting interminable arguments, the broad facts were enough. Here was a prophet who foretold that capitalism, which brought them only toil, poverty and subordination, would surely and certainly destroy itself, had within it the seeds of its own destruction. They, the poor, the workers, the proletariat, were the next class in order of historical succession to be the rulers and controllers. Since they were the last class left, their achievement of power would herald the arrival of a class-less society, and science, engineering and organisation

[1] Where quotations are given, the form used, although the language is occasionally clumsy, is that of the standard English translation.

would produce copious supplies of the material necessities which all would share. Their part was to carry on, energetically and unceasingly, the working-class struggle against the power of capitalism, until the day when its own contradictions decreed its end. Marx became a Messiah in the minds of working men in various parts of Europe, and the latter half of the nineteenth century saw everywhere in Europe the growth of Socialist movements deriving their inspiration from him and striving to formulate their policies and order their activities in conformity with his teaching.

The British working-class movement was perhaps less influenced by his work than any other in the industrially developed countries. Evolutionary theories of social development deriving from Darwin via Herbert Spencer, and propagated by the Fabians led by Sidney Webb, tended to hold the minds of the workers in Britain. Parliamentary democracy, local self-government, trade unionism tended to blur the harsh facts of class domination, class struggle and revolutionary possibilities. Social reforms of one kind and another were conceded to the working class with the same effect. Capitalism progressed, showing no appreciable signs of deterioration, let alone collapse. The avowed Marxists were always a small minority in this country, the Marxist organisations numerically weak ; but pioneers of Labour like Keir Hardie and Robert Smillie, while never speaking in Marxist terms, carried on their varied activities in trade union and political work on the assumption that capitalism was a system carried on in the interest of a greedy, predatory, hostile class, which the workers must organise themselves to fight and finally overthrow. Their leadership also was accepted as of the prophetic order, and their followers also looked forward to the day of salvation and worked for it with religious fervour.

The foregoing, in the most general and all too compressed terms, represents the sociological material available to the young man Lenin in his enforced period of retreat at Kokushkino. For his reading in these years (1888-1890), some fifteen years after the death of Marx, there were available practically all Marx's works, from the Communist Manifesto to the huge *Das Kapital*, together with the writings of Engels and many other disciples and commentators, of whom perhaps the most effective and prolific was Karl Kautsky ; and there was also in existence already, in spite of many obstacles, a native Russian Socialist literature.

IV

LENIN emerged from his banishment in 1891 with his law degree and his Marxist beliefs. It was probably his intention to earn his living as a lawyer and carry on his work for Socialism in his leisure hours. He went to Samara, where he obtained an appointment as an assistant to a barrister, at which post he remained for more than a year. As far as can be gathered, he had little enthusiasm for the work and no notable success, and in 1893 he moved to St. Petersburg and attached himself to the Bar there. Work at the Bar for a livelihood and a compelling urge within him towards Socialist activity proved as incompatible in St. Petersburg as in Samara, and like his teacher Marx, he soon put the law as a career behind him and gave himself unreservedly to the struggle of the workers. His only contact with the law from then onward was to come repeatedly under its ban, until the days when he became the great law-maker of Russia, with an output of a nature unprecedented.

Thus at the age of twenty-three years he stands in St. Petersburg, having thrown the ordinary ambitions of the class from which he had sprung to one side, determined to fight with and for the working class, to look at the world through the eyes of the workers, and to identify himself with their sufferings. He had already, first at Kazan during his banishment and then at Samarkand in his period of law practice, become associated with such Socialist groups as then existed ; he had written one or two pamphlets and theses, and when he came among the Socialists of St. Petersburg he had already some reputation. There was in St. Petersburg greater opportunity both for association with men and women of similar outlook to his own, and for the real educational and organisational activity of a Socialist Movement which his nature demanded. Among his earliest contacts in the city were Nadezhda Konstantinova Krupskaya, who afterwards became his wife and co-worker, and Leonid Krassin, who played a prominent part in the Revolution and the post-revolutionary period of construction, and came to be known in London as Russian Soviet Ambassador.

As in most European countries, the Socialist Movement in Russia at that time was not one compact unified organisation with settled policy and principles. In the period following the emancipation of the peasants large numbers discovered that freedom from serfdom did not realise for them the hopes they had held. Many of the emancipated peasants were landless, many more had holdings too small to produce adequate maintenance, and they were still a class apart without complete civil rights. In 1870 a large number of the youthful intellectuals carried Socialist propaganda in general terms among the peasantry, but made little or no headway. They were confronted by illiteracy, religious superstition and a slave mentality moulded by generations of serfdom. They destroyed their own enthusiasm attempting to beat down these barriers. Turning from their attempt to awaken Socialist thought among the peasant masses, they assumed as their first necessary task the overthrow of Governmental authority as embodied in the Czar. They formed a militant terrorist organisation named ' The People's Will,' and directed their efforts towards terrorist acts against authority and in particular against the Czar. In 1881, in spite of ruthless repression and counter-terrorism by the Government, they succeeded in assassinating Czar Alexander II.

Alexander III., who succeeded him and reigned from 1881 till 1894, carried on a policy of fierce reaction, and the Siberian snows came into steady use as the means to cool revolutionary ardour, while many Socialists went to the scaffold. Socialist activity was driven underground.

In this period the somewhat late capitalist development of Russia began to make up its leeway. Great railway developments took place. Coal and iron mines were opened up, and large sums of foreign capital were attracted into the country for the purposes of industrial development. The liberated but propertyless serfs began to emigrate from their accustomed habitats. A working class of considerable dimensions was now in existence, and the workers were experiencing in their lives the education which comes from associated labour in factory and mine, and which marks out the industrial worker as different from the peasant or the handicraftsman. So there had grown up the beginnings of a population able to assimilate Socialist ideas as formulated in the system of Marx, and groups of Social Democrats had formed to spread those ideas. The old terrorist movement survived from the past ; its members called themselves the Social Revolutionaries, and devoted their attention mainly to the peasantry, to agrarian and land problems, and maintained the individual act of terror as a political method.

Lenin attached himself without hesitation to the Social Democrats, and speedily became one of their foremost controversialists, against the conservatism of the Czar, the nobility and the big landowning interest, against the Liberal politico-social reformism of the merchant, industrial and professional classes, against the mistaken Socialist doctrines of the Social Revolutionaries, and it was not long before he was hotly engaged in controversy inside the party of the Social Democrats itself.

Nicholas II. ascended the throne in 1894, the year when Lenin was establishing himself in the Socialist Movement, and he remained on the throne till 1917, until this Movement, in 1894 only in embryo, surreptitious and underground, had grown to such dimensions, had so gripped the imagination of the Russian masses, that in the appropriate circumstances it swept him—the last of the Romanovs—off the Russian throne and placed in the seat of government Lenin, the Socialist fledgling of 1894.

The difficulties of Socialist propaganda in

Britain in the 'eighties and 'nineties consisted mainly in getting working people to listen. Political discussion was not hampered by legal restriction, and working men who were politically conscious supported the Liberal politicians. In the beginnings of Socialist propaganda they regarded it as something inimical to their trade unions and co-operative societies, and believed that these working-class organisations, assisted by progressive reforms in Parliament, would enable them to achieve the modest improvements in their lives to which they limited their ambitions. Socialists could hold meetings where and when they pleased ; their difficulty was to get people to listen. From 1893 onwards these working-class prejudices and suspicions were steadily broken down, and more and more the public propaganda of Socialism as presented in this country gained the ear of the people.

Conditions for Russian Socialists were quite different, and particularly for Lenin, from whom the eyes of the police were never quite removed from the time of his University trouble. Some of their work was passed by the authorities as legal and was permitted. Lenin regarded this legal work as scarcely worth doing, and concentrated the large proportion of his energies on the underground illegal work, where his statements and expositions did not require to be watered down and emasculated to pass the standards approved by the law. In her *Memories*, Krupskaya casts a light on the methods of work : ' In the autumn of 1894 Vladimir Ilyich read his work *The Friends of the People* to our circle. I remember how everybody scrambled for this book. It set out the aims of our struggle with remarkable clarity. *The Friends of the People* in duplicated form afterwards passed from hand to hand under the alias of the Little Yellow Books. These were unsigned. They had a fairly wide circulation, and there can be no doubt but that they had a strong influence on the Marxist youth of those days.' She continues : ' By the winter of 1894-1895, I had already got to know Vladimir Ilyich fairly intimately.' (Throughout the *Memories* she always refers to Lenin by his baptismal names Vladimir Ilyich or simply Ilyich.) ' He was occupied with the workers' study circles beyond the Nevsky Gate. I had already been working for years in that district as a teacher in the Smolensky Sunday Evening Adult School, and was fairly well acquainted with local working-class life. Quite a number of the workmen in Vladimir Ilyich's circle were my pupils at the Sunday School. In those days the Sunday Evening Adult School was an excellent means for getting a thorough knowledge of the everyday life, the labour conditions and the mood of the working masses. . . . Workers belonging to our organisation went to the School in order to observe the people and note who could be brought into the circles or drawn into the movement. . . . It was a kind of silent conspiracy. We were actually able to talk about anything in the School, although there was rarely a class without a spy. . . . Vladimir Ilyich was interested in the minutest detail describing the conditions and life of the workers. Taking the features separately he endeavoured to grasp the life of the worker as a whole : he tried to find what one could seize upon in order better to approach the worker with revolutionary propaganda. . . . Vladimir Ilyich read with the workers from Marx's *Kapital* and explained it to them. The second half of the studies was devoted to the workers' questions about their work and labour conditions. He showed them how their life was linked up with the entire structure of society, and told them in what manner the existing order could be transformed. . . . The combination of theory with practice was the particular feature of Vladimir

37

Ilyich's work in the circles. Gradually other members of our circle began to use this approach.' These excerpts give some idea of how Lenin did his early Socialist work in St. Petersburg, of how a Socialist organisation began to take form and content, and indicate the roundabout methods that had to be adopted to escape the eye of a vigilant police. Krupskaya describes all the devices of secrecy they had to adopt : how a serious meeting would meet under the innocent title of a ' pancake tea ' ; how devious routes had to be taken to dodge police spies in approaching and leaving their gatherings ; how they had recourse to the use of invisible ink and ciphers. In this way and in the writing of some pamphlets for the workers on ' The Law of Fines,' ' The New Factory Act,' ' On Strikes,' and ' On Industrial Courts,' where his legal knowledge was made to serve his Socialist purposes, he spent his time until the year 1895.

He had a bad illness in that year, and in the summer obtained permission to go abroad to recover his health. His idea of convalescing was to go to Berlin and attend workers' meetings, and to Switzerland, where at Geneva he met Plekhanov, Axelrod and Vera Sassulich, the recognised leaders of Russian Social Democracy in exile, known as the Emancipation of Labour Group.

His meeting with Plekhanov provided him with new plans and ideas for future work, and he returned from Geneva with a trunk full of illegal literature, with a plan for a Socialist newspaper, and even with the printing press necessary to produce it. To get these over the frontier was a work of difficulty. He got down at once to the task of producing the newspaper. It was given the title ' The Workmen's Cause ' (*Rabocheye Delo*), and was intended to appear at the beginning of December 1895. Everything was in order and the proofs corrected, when the staff, including Lenin, disappeared. The police had penetrated their secrets, or perhaps their eagerness for their new venture had made them neglect their usual precautions, but the enterprise was nipped in the bud and Lenin saw for the first time the inside of prison walls.

V

IMPRISONMENT of active members was so common a feature of Russian Socialist life that arrangements for carrying on the work of the prisoner and for establishing communication with him were always ready. Political prisoners were permitted a limited number of letters and might receive supplies of books from their friends outside. These had, of course, to pass a censorship, but invisible ink, codes, ciphers and dotted letters made it possible to communicate important information both in and out. It may also be concluded that just as police spies found their way into workers' circles, so among prison officers would be found sometimes one not unsympathetic to the political prisoners, and perhaps also several who were not averse to adding to their meagre incomes in return for services rendered, or for the turning of a blind eye at the right moment. In any case the personality of Lenin forced itself most effectively through the prison walls for the encouragement of his comrades in other cells and for the stimulation of the activity of those who remained at liberty, and the movement went on.

He spent his term of imprisonment in solitary confinement ; but with the help of books from outside, a prison cell was not a bad place for the work of serious literary production to a man whose health could stand the rigours of prison life, and whose mental attitude made him independent of luxurious food or furnishings. He proceeded to prepare his book on *The Development of Capitalism in Russia*, and made substantial progress. His imprisonment, or preliminary detention, as it was more euphoniously termed, lasted for one year, until the Czar was ready to pronounce sentence, which took the form of banishment to Siberia for three years. When Lenin heard of this decision he remarked in jest : ' It is a pity they let us out so soon. I would have liked to do a little more work on the book. It will be difficult to obtain books in Siberia.' During his imprisonment his Socialist comrades had played an active part in a big strike of weavers ; many of them found their way also into prison, and before he came out Krupskaya was in. She therefore had no opportunity of seeing him before his departure for Siberia, but she seems to have gained some satisfaction from the information that he had grown fatter as a result of his imprisonment.

In January 1897 he proceeded to Siberia. The place fixed for him to live was the village of Shushenskoye, in the district of Minussinsk on the river Yenisei. Krupskaya's *Memories* provide a very vivid description of the life of the political exile in that area. She followed him there after a year, having herself been sentenced to three years' exile in another place. She, describing herself as his fiancée (which was a little in advance of the fact), requested and was granted permission to join him at Shushenskoye. Her mother accompanied her into exile in May 1898. She describes their arrival at the peasant's log-house where Lenin was living, and draws a picture of the interior of the typical house. ' The peasants are particularly clean in their habits. The floors are covered with brightly coloured home-spun mats, the walls whitewashed and decorated with fir branches. The room used by Vladimir Ilyich, though not large, was spotlessly clean. My mother and I were given the remaining part of the cottage.'

Lenin was out shooting at the time of her arrival, and during his exile this was his chief recreation. Hares and wild-duck were the principal game, and he possessed a Gordon setter of fine qualities which he had thoroughly trained in the duties of a sporting dog. Here we get glimpses of his lighter side, see him playing with children and joining with fellow exiles and their families in the lusty singing of choruses. He was also a great enthusiast for chess, a game he had played at home as a boy. Winter brought them unlimited opportunity for skating on the frozen river. His chief indoor recreation was reading philosophy, Hegel, Kant and the French naturalists, Pushkin, Lermontov and Nekrassov, and he also read the fiction of Turgeniev, Tolstoy and Chernyshevsky. But the student, writer and working-class leader overshadowed all else, and work filled most of his hours. He lived during his exile on a subvention of eight roubles, which kept him in food, board, laundry and mending. The peasants with whom he boarded had frequent drinking bouts, which made it difficult for him to find peace for his work, and the three of them therefore removed to a part of a house which they hired for themselves for four roubles. To this was attached a garden which provided them with another recreation and also with fresh vegetables. He completed the book he had begun in prison on *The Development of Capitalism in Russia*, and wrote *The Tasks of the Russian Social Democrats*. With Krupskaya he translated *The History of Trade Unionism*, by Sidney and Beatrice Webb, from English into Russian, although when they came to England some time later, he confessed that he was unable to understand one word of the language as spoken.

In February 1900 his exile came to an end, and he was free to return to Russia. He was now a man of thirty years, and for four years he had been forcibly prevented from participating personally in the active life of the Russian Socialist Movement, but among his fellow-exiles and the local inhabitants of his exile home he had sowed the seeds of his revolutionary theory, continued his study of the working-class and peasant mind at first hand, and maintained contact with the wider Movement by continuous and systematic correspondence. It was at this time that he began to use his name, N. Lenin, as a *nom de guerre*.

During his exile in Siberia, the development of capitalist industry in Russia led to some strikes which were successful in securing some concessions to the workers, and led to a tendency among the Social Democrats to argue that Socialists should leave political action alone and concentrate on industrial action. The supporters of this view came to be known by the name of ' Economists,' and for a time theirs was the predominating voice among the Russian Social Democrats. At intervals the Socialist movements of other European countries has been influenced by the same view, and it has indeed always held the field in the American working-class movement. On Lenin's return from exile he set himself to combat and counteract this tendency.

He was not permitted to return to St. Petersburg, but was allowed to live at Pskov, which was not the ideal centre for him, but was a vast improvement on prison and Siberia. He paid a visit to St. Petersburg in June of that year with his comrade Martov. They were followed by the police and arrested, but after ten days' detention they were liberated.

A Conference of the revolutionary wing of the Social Democrats, held at Pskov about this time, decided that Lenin, Martov and Potresov should go abroad and re-establish contact with Plekhanov and his group in exile, with a view to resurrecting their newspaper project which had been so abruptly terminated four years previously. Before leaving, Lenin paid a fleeting visit to Krupskaya, whose term of exile had not yet expired, and who was now living at Ufa. He also visited his mother at Podolsk, and then, on 29th July 1900, he proceeded abroad by way of Prague to Munich.

His wife Krupskaya followed him some months later, and has given an amusing account of her difficulties in tracing him on account of the insufficient information of his whereabouts given her, and the care he had taken to cover his tracks against other and less desirable pursuers. Their life abroad opens up a new and important phase in his development.

VI

Lenin arrived in Munich with his plans and
ideas for his future work well defined in his
mind. The Russian Social Democrats had to
be welded into a party with a Marxist revolutionary basis and definite methods of working.
Many groups existed in different parts of
Russia, some of them federated in localities,
but there was as yet no All Russian organisation
with a common centre and a recognised leadership. A Conference held at Minsk in 1898,
with the aim of securing the basis necessary for
an organisation of national scope, was badly
handicapped through the fact that the persons
most necessary for its success were in prison or
in exile. Only some eight or nine delegates
attended, and they were not able to do much
more than issue a Manifesto, declare the formation of the Russian Social Democratic Labour
Party, and recognise the *Rabochaya Gazeta* as the
Party organ. The intellectual leadership of
the Russian Marxist Movement was taken by
what was known as the Emancipation of

Labour Group, consisting of George Plekhanov, Vera Sassulich and Paul Axelrod, of whom Plekhanov was the acknowledged leader. Although in the year 1900 he was only a man of forty-two years of age, he was regarded as the father and founder of Russian Marxism, and Lenin looked up to him with almost filial respect. The other two members of the group were also middle-aged. All three had been exiles since 1883, and were known only through their writings to the younger generation to which Lenin belonged.

Lenin's first object was to establish close relationship with this group, renewing the contact he had made with them on his brief visit in 1895, and to develop anew the project for a newspaper which had failed through the action of the authorities five years earlier. On this occasion the publication of the paper was to be done abroad. The preliminary negotiations between the two groups raised difficulties both of temperament and policy, which threatened to wreck the venture at the outset, and Lenin's uncritical regard for Plekhanov was somewhat reduced. Means were found for overcoming the difficulties, at least for a time, and the scheme for the newspaper went ahead. The differences between the two groups had

crystallised round the question of editorial
control. Plekhanov and his associates were
living at Geneva, while Lenin and his friends
had fixed Munich as their headquarters. In
the arrangement finally reached an editorial
board was to control the paper, and it was
agreed to print it at Munich. Lenin's wife
was to act as editorial secretary, a position
which in the peculiar circumstances in which
they had to work meant that she acted as
circulation manager and Party secretary as
well ; so that it can easily be seen that the
effective control rested mainly in the hands of
Lenin, both as regards the direction of the
policy of the paper and the organisation of the
Party.

The name given to the new journal was
Iskra (The Spark), and it was decided that a
companion publication, devoted more to the
theoretical aspects of Socialism and entitled
Zarya (The Dawn), should be produced under
the same direction. A declaration by the
Editorial Board of the two journals gives a
clear idea of the policy to be pursued : ' The
practical conclusion to be drawn from all this
is as follows : We Russian Social-Democrats
must combine and direct all our efforts towards
the formation of a strong Party which must lead

the struggle under the united banner of revolutionary Social-Democracy. This is precisely the task that was outlined by the Congress in 1898, at which the Russian Social-Democratic Labour Party was formed and which published its Manifesto. We regard ourselves as members of this Party ; we entirely agree with the fundamental ideas contained in the Manifesto, and attach extreme importance to it as a public declaration of its aims. Consequently we as members of the Party present the question as to what our immediate and direct tasks are, as follows. What plan of activity must we adopt in order to revive the Party on the firmest possible basis ? The reply usually made to this question is that it is necessary to elect a central party institution once more, and to instruct that body to resume publication of the Party organ. But in the confused period through which we are now passing such a simple method is hardly adequate.

' To establish and consolidate the Party means to establish and consolidate unity among all Russian Social-Democrats, and for the reasons indicated above, such unity cannot be brought about by simply giving orders ; it cannot be brought about by, let us say, a meeting of representatives passing resolutions.

Definite work must be done to bring it about.
In the first place it is necessary to bring about
unity of ideas, which will remove the differences of opinion and confusion that—we will
be frank—reign among Social-Democrats at
the present time.

'This unity of ideas must be fortified by
a unified party programme. Secondly, an
organisation must be set up, especially for the
purpose of maintaining contact among all the
centres of the movement, for supplying complete and timely information about the movement, and for supplying it regularly to the
periodical press in all parts of Russia. Only
when we have established such an organisation, only when we have established a Russian
Socialist postal system, will the Party have a
chance of permanent existence, and only then
will it become a real factor and consequently
a mighty political force.'

The Editors proceed further to state the
necessity of open discussion in the columns of
the papers if intellectual unity is to be secured :
'Open polemics within the sight and hearing
of all Russian Social-Democrats and class conscious workers are necessary and desirable, in
order to explain the profound differences that
exist, to obtain a comprehensive discussion of

disputed question, and to combat the extremes into which not only the representatives of various views, but also of various localities or various " crafts " in the revolutionary movement inevitably fall.'

This declaration was published as a separate leaflet for distribution in September 1900. Although issued in the name of the Editorial Board, it is a Lenin production, and so we find him at the age of thirty years in a central position in the Russian Socialist Movement, from which he aimed to mould its thought, unify the various fragments of its organisation, and direct its efforts towards no less an end than the complete overthrow of Czarism and the economic system that maintained itself under Czarism. Only seventeen years were to pass before he saw his object achieved. They were for him years of incessant toil, spent almost wholly in exile, except for a short period in 1905-1907, when the upheaval of 1905 made his return to Russia possible.

In Munich, as leading editor of *Iskra*, he lived the same simple Spartan life that was his regular habit. He and his wife lived in a small house in the Schwabing suburb of Munich which they had furnished themselves. The nature of this establishment may be gathered from Krupskaya's remark in her *Memories*, 'We sold it all for twelve marks when we left.' He made no attempt to take part in the life and work of the Social Democratic Party in Germany, but occasionally attended meetings, saw the May Day Demonstration in 1901, and met one or two of the leaders, notably Rosa Luxemburg, who met her death along with Karl Liebknecht as a result of the Spartacist revolt in Germany after the war. His opportunities for outdoor recreation were more limited than in Siberia, he got no skating, no hunting, only quiet rambles in desolate spots on the outskirts of Munich, where fresh air could be had without interrupting the work of thinking.

His journalistic output during this period was very great, and no article was written for any purpose but to serve the one great end. Among the most important of his articles was one which appeared in May 1901, in the fourth issue of *Iskra*, entitled 'Where to Begin.' This article was expanded into a book, which came out in 1902 under the title *What is to be Done?* and is regarded as the authoritative statement of the policy of Russian Social Democracy.

His articles covered a wide range, including 'The Chinese War,' 'Casual Notes,' in which he exposes a revolting case of the maltreatment of prisoners in Russian prisons, ' The Theory of Rent,' ' Machinery in Agriculture,' ' The Productivity of Small and Large Farms,' ' The Russian Budget of 1902.'

In addition to all this, he carried on a steady controversy with the Economist wing of the Party, which had managed to establish a paper under the old title of Lenin's first venture, the *Rabocheye Delo* (The Workmen's Cause). An attempt was made to bring about unity between the groups around the two journals, but a meeting held at Zurich with this object in October 1901 failed to produce the desired result.

In the early part of 1902 it became impossible to continue producing *Iskra* in Munich, as the printer there was afraid any longer to run the risk involved. This was a severe blow. The organisation for introducing the paper into Russia and into circulation there was just getting into working order. Every batch of the paper had to be smuggled over the frontier, had to reach reliable hands in the various districts and from them pass into secret circulation. All the information, names and addresses necessary to this task were in the care of Krupskaya, who maintained communications and interviewed the emissaries who from time to time came from Russia. The whole organisation radiated from Munich, and a change of centre entailed big readjustments.

There was some dispute among the members of the Board as to where they should go. Plekhanov and Axelrod favoured Switzerland, the rest voted for London, and to London they went, arriving there in April 1902.

VII

Lenin's life in London did not differ in its essence from his life in prison, in Siberia or in Munich. His concentration on his revolutionary purpose so possessed him that one thinks of him as going through life only half conscious of his surroundings, realising and noticing only those phenomena which had a bearing on his work. His wife always made the arrangements about where they should live and the manner of the domestic life. He required only a place where he could pace back and forward, a desk to write at and a chair to sit on. Never do we find him becoming involved in social associations of any permanent kind. Other members of the *Iskra* group tended to herd together and share rooms; Lenin and his wife kept to themselves. She liked to have charge of his food herself. With reference to their life in London she says: ' Soon my mother was due to arrive, and we decided to live in family style, that is, to hire two rooms and eat at home. For we had found that the

Russian stomach is not easily adaptable to the
' ox-tails,' skate fried in fat, cake and other
mysteries of English fare. What is more, we
were at that time on the pay-roll of our organisation, which meant that we had to look after
every penny and live as cheaply as possible.'
When the Party was in funds, £6 per month
was Lenin's salary, so the economies of his
wife were not without compulsion. The house
they occupied was at 30 Holford Square, a not
very inspiring quarter in the area lying to the
north of Euston Road. It did not have any
special advantages, except that it was situated
between the British Museum and Highgate
Cemetery, where Karl Marx was buried.

In Munich the couple had lived under the
name of Meyer. Here in London they assumed the name of Richter. In those days
London knew little or nothing of passport
restrictions or registration of aliens, and was a
real asylum for political refugees. So far as
British conditions were concerned, they might
quite well have used his family name of
Ul'yanov or his political name of Lenin with
impunity, but the Russian Government had a
long arm. Russia was then experiencing a
period of political activity on the part of the
elements working for political democracy,

accompanied by a reign of terror on the part of Nicholas II. and his Ministers, Stolypin and Witte. Massacres of the Jewish population took place systematically, the hated Black Hundred acted as a brutal agent of reaction, and secret police spies were to be found everywhere and in every organisation. Carelessness on the part of one member of an organisation might lead to the death or imprisonment of many. The care with which Lenin concealed his identity was no mere stage trick, but an absolutely necessary precaution for the safety of his lieutenants and followers in Russia itself.

The British Museum Reading-room was a favourite haunt and working place. Its library resources fascinated him, and his later visit to London was made in order to have the benefit of the volumes there. It had also been the favourite laboratory of Karl Marx. The professor and staff of the Physics and Natural Philosophy Department of Glasgow University used to state with pride that the great Atlantic cable which established telegraphic communication between Europe and America was laid from their laboratories by the eminent scientist who later became the famous Lord Kelvin. At some date in the future the authorities of the British Museum may take pride in the fact that two great pioneers of a new world civilisation worked out their plans within the walls of the Museum. But that time has not yet arrived.

Lenin and his wife both found their book-learned English inadequate to the purpose of effective work in London, and immediately set themselves to get a practical working knowledge of the language. One of their favourite ways of learning was to listen to the open-air orators at Hyde Park, but Lenin also entered into an arrangement for exchange lessons with an Englishman desiring to learn Russian, and speedily acquired sufficient facility to get on with his work.

He was greatly impressed by the variety of London life, by the evidences of great wealth and great poverty side by side. Krupskaya mentions in her book how in face with these contrasts she heard him muttering through his clenched teeth, and in English, ' Two nations,' which seems to indicate a lapse from the natural Marxist form of ' Two classes ' into a form made familiar by Disraeli.

In this summer Lenin took the first holiday recorded in his adult life. His mother was living in Brittany, and he joined her there for a month by the sea ; but it may easily be believed that he took his thoughts and his plans with him.

Shortly after he returned from this holiday, Trotsky arrived in London, having escaped from exile in Siberia, and the first meeting of these two men who were to figure so prominently in momentous happenings took place at an early hour in the morning in Lenin's London home. Trotsky in his book, *Lenin*, describes the event : ' I arrived in London in the autumn of 1902. It must have been in October, and early in the morning. A cab that I engaged because I saw others doing so took me to an address jotted down on a scrap of paper—my destination. This was Vladimir Ilyich's home. Before this (it must have been in Zurich) I had been taught to knock at a door in a certain definite way. As far as I remember, Nadezhda Konstantinova (Madame Lenin) opened the door for me ; I had fetched her out of bed with my knocking, as one can imagine. It was early in the morning, and any sensible man more familiar with the ordinary conventions of life, would have waited an hour or two at the station, instead of knocking at strange doors at dawn. But I was still completely under the influence of my flight from

Vercholensk.[1] I had already roused Axelrod's household in Zurich in the same way, only not at dawn but in the middle of the night. Vladimir Ilyich was still in bed, and he greeted me with justifiable surprise. Under such conditions our first meeting and our first conversation took place.' They became immediately immersed in a discussion about the progress of their ideas in Russia, and Lenin found in Trotsky at once a comrade whom he liked. In subsequent Party disputes they found themselves in opposition on important issues, but in the critical period of revolutionary activity in 1917 they worked hand in hand, and Lenin entrusted Trotsky with the control of work which was vital to the success of the Revolution.

In London the work of producing *Iskra* and *Zarya* went on, with the control largely in the hands of Lenin. Neither Plekhanov nor Axelrod had removed their homes from Switzerland to London with the removal of the paper's headquarters there, but they came over for consultation and discussion. Vera Sassulich, Martov and Blumenfeld lived together, and Trotsky found accommodation with them. Blumenfeld was not a member of the Editorial

[1] Trotsky had come almost direct to London after escaping from exile at Vercholensk in Siberia.

Board, but concerned himself solely with the
technical work of printing, publication, and
despatch. There was a demand that Trotsky
should return to Russia and engage in the
organisational work there, but Lenin preferred
that he should remain in London for a period,
and he became one of the contributors to *Iskra*.

About this time preparations were afoot for
getting together a real Party Congress. To
English political people, used to their annual
conferences and monthly meetings of large
party councils, the idea of a party continuing
in active being from 1898 till 1903 without any
conference, without any central council other
than the board of a newspaper, is a matter for
wonder. Again the conditions of Russian life
and the vast extent of Russia itself must be
borne in mind. The work of preparing for the
Conference fell to the *Iskra* staff, and included
the arrangement of the place of conference,
communicating with the different groups who
would send delegates, and above all, the drafting of a Party programme which should state
in more precise terms the Party objects, till
then only expressed in general terms in the
Manifesto of the 1898 Conference with its eight
delegates. In November 1902 an Organising
Committee for the preparation of the Congress

was constituted in Russia, but in the conditions ruling, Lenin had to a large extent to organise these organisers. The drafting of the programme fell naturally into his hands, with Plekhanov as critic and amender. There was constant controversy between them as to the presentation of the programme, Lenin being in favour of very great precision of language, while Plekhanov preferred the inclusion of those useful qualifying phrases which politicians at all times and in all places find so useful. Trotsky indicates the nature of the differences between the two leaders : ' In the organising political work Lenin wanted to be as independent as possible of the old men, of Plekhanov above all, with whom he had already had sharp conflicts, especially in perfecting the draft of the Party programme. . . . I only learned gradually of the sharp clashes between Lenin and Plekhanov in the management of the theoretical part of the programme. . . . The differences of opinion concerned the policy of greater sharpness and exactitude in characterising the chief tendencies of capitalism, the concentration of production, the disintegration of the intermediate ranks, the class differences, etc., on Lenin's side, and on greater consideration of conditions and caution on the

63

part of Plekhanov. The programme, as is well known, abounds in the words " more or less " ; that is due to Plekhanov. The struggle assumed a very dramatic form. Vera Ivan-ovna (Sassulich) said to Lenin as she told the story, " George (Plekhanov) is a greyhound. He shakes and shakes the adversary and lets him go ; but you are a bull-dog, you have a deadly bite." ' Substantial agreement on the programme was ultimately reached between them, so that when the Conference arrived they were its joint defenders.

This struggle, combined with the conditions of his life in London, had produced bad effects on Lenin's health, and he got into a very nervous state, suffering much from sleeplessness. About the same time all the members of the staff except himself wished to remove the head-quarters from London to Switzerland, and he fell in with the wish of the majority. While they were preparing for the move Lenin's nervous troubles took an acute turn. Krups-kaya, because she had been told that medical attention in London would cost a guinea, acted as his doctor with the aid of a medical hand-book and with the assistance of one of their Russian friends who had been a medical student. The principal symptom was inflammation of the nerve terminals of back and chest, which she describes as ' holy fire ' or ' shearers' rash.' Her remedy was to paint the affected part with iodine. In this condition he set out on his journey to Geneva, but on arrival there collapsed completely, and had to lie in bed for a fortnight.

Thus ended his first stay in London. As in Munich he took no part in the German Socialist Movement, so in London his contact with the British Socialist Movement was slight ; but he liked to go to the Socialist churches then in existence, where a Socialist meeting was conducted with all the usual forms of a church service, sermon, reading of lessons, singing of hymns and sometimes even prayer. Such a thing was a new phenomenon to him.

VIII

In April 1903 the Lenin family group took up residence in Séchéron, a working-class quarter of Geneva. Their house here was on a similar scale to those they had occupied in London and Munich, the kitchen having to serve as the room for receiving visitors, and the cases that had conveyed their goods and chattels on the journey having to form an important part of the furniture.

The date of the much-longed-for Congress was now at hand, and although it was to take place at Brussels, delegates were already beginning to turn up both from Russia and other parts of Europe, and were reporting themselves at Geneva. Many informal discussions took place over matters in dispute. Not only was the power of the *Iskra* group resented by certain sections coming from Russia, but the divisions among the Iskra-ites themselves were acute on certain issues. There were in all fifty-seven delegates, not an imposing array judged by later standards, but compared with the eight

of the first Congress of 1898, sufficiently large
to encourage Lenin in the belief that progress
was being made. Only forty-three of the delegates had full voting powers. The Congress
started in Brussels in a big flour warehouse,
specially decorated with red bunting for the
occasion, and the first parts of the proceedings
were carried through there. Then the Belgian
authorities began to interfere with the delegates
and deported two of them, and the Congress
decided to remove to London. There it did
its work without interference from outside but
with much acrimony within.

The big issue involved and underlying most
of the questions under discussion as well as
affecting the elections to important positions
in the Party was one which, at that time, was
the subject of controversy in every European
Socialist Party, and in the Conferences of the
International Socialist Movement. It was
usually called the fight between Revisionism or
Reformism and Revolution. The Revisionist
view had received theoretical formulation at
the hands of Eduard Bernstein, the German
Social Democrat, who had enunciated a revised
statement of Marxism tending to present the
progress to Socialism as a slow evolutionary
development rather than as a violent clash of

classes in revolutionary conflict. It challenged the conception of a capitalist system reaching a stage of collapse, and visualised it rather as progressing steadily into a higher form of social organisation, aided by the intelligent guidance and influence of Socialist thought and Socialist movements. The revolutionary view had as its foremost European exponent Karl Kautsky, who hotly combated the teaching of Bernstein.

The German Social Democratic Party, under the influence of its powerful leader Auguste Bebel, decided in favour of the revolutionary view, but made its decisions in such a form as to avoid any split in their Party. The subsequent history of the German Party seems to show that the real victory was with the Revisionist, Reformist and Evolutionary elements which have usually dominated the tactics of German Socialism ; but the tradition of one united disciplined Party accepting the will of the majority has been maintained since, accompanied by splits on the left wing when the Reformist view of the majority became intolerable to the revolutionary members in face of critical issues.

In France the same difference of opinion also appeared, but took other forms. As early as 1899, Millerand, taking the Reformist view, had entered a French Liberal Cabinet, but he and his supporters were expelled from the Socialist Party in 1904. In the history of French Socialism this association with non-Socialist Governments became quite a recognised and established practice, Briand and Viviani being notable examples of men who, starting in the Socialist Movement, came to be members and leaders of non-Socialist administrations.

Italy, Belgium, Australia and Britain all reproduced the same phenomenon, John Burns being the person who pioneered the practice here. In every place where Socialists congregate, a discussion on this question can still arise at any time, and the decisions of Socialist Parties and individuals in any given situation are largely governed by the side they take on this issue.

Lenin had very early in his Socialist thinking made up his mind on the subject. He had seen the difficulties that had arisen in other countries by the evasion of hard decisions on the question, and had made up his mind that so far as he was concerned there would be no evasions nor postponements of a difficulty. He could see that a different character was necessary for a Party which took the revolutionary road, a different form of organisation, a different type of member and a different type of service from the member, than was required along the peaceful road of evolutionary Socialism. For the first was required a man or woman who was prepared to ' shun delights and live laborious days,' to make every waking thought and act subserve his revolutionary purpose. He must be ready to give up father, mother, wife or child, and to live by the principle that ' the cause alone was worthy.' He would carry neither purse nor scrip. He had to carry his life and his liberty in his hands. The applause and the approval of the multitudes were not for him. The gate of entry must be strait and the way narrow until the day of liberation, when the faithful disciple would find an ample reward in seeing the achievement of his Socialist purpose.

For the Reformist the road opened out a different vista. The development of capitalist industry would lead to a progressive amelioration of working-class life. Increased production would become possible through improved forms of organisation. A Socialist Party would depict the Socialist Commonwealth as the culminating stage of this progress. The necessities of capitalism itself would compel the establishment of democratic forms of government and make the absolute rule of Czars or Kaisers impossible. The Socialist Party taking this view would assist other progressive elements in hastening the democratic process. When representative governing institutions were achieved its members would contest electorally for a share in the representation, would agitate for improvements in working-class life, and show incidentally how economic development could only be perfected in a Socialist form. Such a political theory did not call for heroic or Spartan characters ; unless in countries of black tyranny like Russia it did not call for conspiratorial methods. It could make a wide appeal to all sorts and conditions of men. It offered prospects of a career to the ambitious, and did not make of its adherents outcasts on the face of the earth. Neither did it call for a strict discipline nor precise definition of aims and methods. The gulf between those who held such a Socialist view and Liberals with a taste for social reform was not so wide but that it could always be bridged when opportunity offered.

The individuals who best typified this attitude in the ranks of Russian Social Democracy at that time were P. V. Struve and M. Tugan-Baranovsky, both of whom ceased to have any connection with the Party after 1905, when they became members of the Liberal Party, or Cadets as they were called. At the time of this Congress they represented the extreme right-wing view and had only a negligible following in the Party. But Lenin was very alert for any indication of this tendency, in however modified a form, among the delegates, and in his preparation of the programme endeavoured to get a formulation that would make such an attitude impossible inside the Party organisation. To him Revolution meant Revolution, Class War meant Class War, Socialism meant Socialism, and he was not of a mind to smooth off the rough edges, nor to make the way easy for waverers and the weaker brethren. He believed that the road to Socialism for Russia would be a hard one, and he wanted no one to set out on it who would faint and fall by the way. He had laid down his position with great clarity in *Iskra* in the article ' Where to Begin,' and had elaborated it still further in his book *What is to be Done ?* These writings had been thoroughly circulated and fully canvassed among the active spirits of the Party.

Paragraph I. of the Statutes of the Party, defining the qualifications for membership, gave the opportunity for a full debate as between the two tendencies. Lenin desired a form of words that would limit membership to those who put themselves, body and soul, into the organisation and under its direction. The leading spokesman for the opposing view was Martov, who favoured a less hard formulation which, in Lenin's opinion, opened the door to every form of opportunism. In spite of the support of Plekhanov, on this issue Lenin was defeated.

On the next important vote he secured a majority. He proposed that in addition to the Central Committee of the Party in Russia, a second headquarters should be set up abroad, which should carry on the publication of the *Iskra* and be the supreme authority. This proposal was carried by 25 votes of the majority to 23 of the minority. The Russian words Bolsheviki (majority) and Mensheviki (minority) took on a new significance from the time of this vote, first in Russian political controversy, and then in world affairs. It is interesting to ponder the connotation of the word Bolshevik in the minds of statesmen, capitalists and workers everywhere in comparison with its simple significance at this unimposing Congress in 1903.

IX

THIS Second Congress and its results may well have produced in the mind of Lenin that mistrust of ' formal democracy,' as he termed it, which became a distinctive part of his political mentality. He learned here in practice that to secure a majority vote on given issues did not confer power, nor did it by any means settle those issues finally and for ever. In the period following the Revolution of 1917, the way in which he brushed aside the ordinary machinery of democracy, elections, voting, majority decisions, representative assemblies, came as a shock to those who had become accustomed to regard the machinery through which it operated as democracy itself. No sooner was the London Congress over, having appointed Lenin, Plekhanov and Martov as its Editorial Board and highest central authority, than his troubles began. Martov declined to act in the Triumvirate. Further, although the policy pursued by *Iskra* had been approved, the Menshevik section did not believe in it, and did not propose to leave Lenin in the central position of power, from which he could disseminate his revolutionary ideas. Plekhanov laboured to find a compromise that would prevent a split in the Party. He proposed to co-opt the former members of the Editorial Board. Lenin resigned from the Board, stating that he would cease collaborating, but did not wish it to be announced that his resignation was the result of differences of policy. A month or two later he resigned also from the Central Committee. All attempts to find a working compromise failed. The Menshevik point of view was in the ascendant so far as those outside Russia were concerned, and Lenin, after his strenuous years of preparation, found himself well outside the central councils of the Party. He wrote a pamphlet, ' One step forward, two steps back,' a title which summarised his view of the amount of progress made at the Congress.

He was now at a loose end, out of a job, without a fulcrum on which he could rest his lever. With Krupskaya, his faithful wife and companion, he set off for a tramp among the Swiss mountains. Even then, he carried with him something to work on. Krupskaya tells that their rucksacks were loaded, hers with a

French book which she was translating, his with a French dictionary ; but they were never taken out on the journey. They spent a month in the mountains. Lenin found peace for his disheartened and troubled spirit among the hills, and gathered momentum for a new effort. The view of the mountains put his troubles in a better perspective. A further month was spent with some of his friends and supporters in an obscure village by the side of Lac de Bré. Here they planned out a newspaper to further the Bolshevik position in the Party and to agitate for the summoning of another Congress. On their return to Geneva at the end of this holiday, he settled down to his old systematic method of work, using the library of the Société de Lecture as his workshop. The new paper was named *Vpered* (Forward), and in its columns he proceeded once more to enunciate the policy which he wholeheartedly believed was the only possible one for Russian Socialists, but which, so far, Russian Socialists were disinclined to accept.

From this time the two wings, Bolshevik and Menshevik, existed nominally in the same Party, the Russian Social Democratic Labour Party, but the Bolsheviks had their own independent organ, and their own organisation, and as time passed, the lines of demarcation became more clearly defined, although members passed at various times and on various issues from the one group to the other. None of Lenin's former intimates supported him at this time, and his main support in his new venture, *Vpered*, came from Lunarcharsky, who after the Revolution became Commissar of Education, and Bogdanov, with whom he had formed a friendship in the London days. They got together something in the nature of a Conference, appointed a new Central Committee, and developed their machinery for contact with Russia. For Lenin the best part of a year had been consumed in clearing up the aftermath of the Congress, in getting back his health and spirits, and in establishing a new base of operations.

It so happened that just when the dispute between the two wings of the Party had reached such an acute stage, events in Russia began to develop in a way that presented opportunities for work. Czar Nicholas was also having his troubles. He plunged the nation into the war with Japan over Korea in January 1904. From the outset all the politically conscious elements in Russia (outside immediately Czarist circles) were in complete hostility to the adventure.

If success had crowned his efforts, it is likely that the Liberal capitalists would have applauded and proceeded to exploit the people and resources of Korea, but the campaign was a complete disaster. The equipment of the army was poor, the generalship indifferent, transport was a matter of constant difficulty, and above all the nation was not behind the Czar and his armies. After the decisive defeats of the Russian army at Mukden and of the navy at Shushima in the early months of 1905, Russia sued for peace, which was concluded in September of that year.

During the progress of the war, in an endeavour to conciliate a public opinion which was more than usually vocal in its discontent, and with the hope of buying off the again active terrorists, the Czar appointed a Ministry of Liberal outlook, which made certain concessions, including a measure of liberty to the press. The press made full use of their liberty, and the Czar learned exactly where he stood in the hearts of his people. Hunger and hardship prevailed amongst the mass of the working people, and the feelings aroused by privation were finding expression. As a means of combating the spread of revolutionary ideas, Unions under the aegis of Government agents were

formed, but even these artificial products became centres of discontent.

On 22nd January 1905 a peaceful demonstration of the poorest citizens, headed by the
priest, Father Gapon, and carrying religious
emblems, marched to the Winter Palace to
present a humble petition to the Czar to take
pity on their sufferings. The Czar was ready
to receive them. His troops were drawn up in
order, and when the procession was in position,
the order to fire was given. Two hundred of
these poverty-stricken people were slaughtered.
These were no revolutionaries. They had come
only to beg relief of their miseries. Their
leader, so far from being a Socialist, was in
reality a tool of the police. 22nd January 1905
has gone down to history as 'Red Sunday.'
One can imagine how the realist mind and
revolutionary temper of Lenin reacted when
the news of this bloody outrage reached him
at Geneva.

Further news of the stirrings of revolt came
from remote corners of Russia. 'Now,' said
this expert theorist of revolution, 'we have
some practical experience by which to support
and test our theories.' He did not regard this
outbreak of 1905 as the revolution for which
he was waiting and working, but he did expect

it to carry the people some part of the road, and to develop in them the class consciousness which was essential to the bigger effort. Its result further impressed upon him the folly of leading unarmed and untrained masses of people against drilled and equipped soldiers, still loyal to the ruling caste. From then on-wards he became steadily more insistent on the necessity for the armed insurrection, for the proper preparation of the minds of the mass of the people, for the training of the leaders and for the wooing of the soldiers from their allegiance.

The new situation arising from the spirit of revolt now abroad in Russia was one from which he felt he could not be absent, but as yet it was not possible for him to return. Russia, however, came to him. Soon there arrived at Geneva Father Gapon. His part in the demonstration at the Winter Palace had led to his speedy exodus from Russia. The Social Democrats abroad had no very great belief in Gapon as a leader of working-class revolt. Their anti-clerical instincts were all against him, and the rumour that he had been to some extent the catspaw of the Govern-ment had possibly reached them through their channels of information. To Lenin, however, he was a man fresh from the scene of action. He had been a central figure in a great historical event, and Lenin wished to learn all that was to be learned of this event. He met him, talked with him, questioned him. On 8th February 1905 he wrote in *Vpered* : ' We hope George Gapon, who has experienced and felt so profoundly the transition from the opinions of a politically unconscious people to revolutionary views, will succeed in working to obtain that clarity of revolutionary outlook necessary for a political leader.'

Under the influence of these events, before he left Geneva he included in his reading a study of works on the technique of war and military tactics. In conjunction with Gapon he set about the organisation of a supply of arms to the Fighting Committee of the Bolsheviks, and just as the British Museum helped to arm Lenin theoretically, so Britain was the source from which the supply of arms was drawn. They did not, however, reach their destination, the plans for their transport proving unsatisfactory : but through the capable business management of Krassin, large supplies of arms did find their way into the hands of the revolutionaries, and Lenin wrote articles urging the necessity for a disciplined striking force. The St. Petersburg Social Democrats belonged to the Bolshevik wing, and they issued on the day after the massacre a manifesto of hot denunciation. ' Citizens,' it read, ' yesterday you saw the brutality of the absolutist government ! You saw the blood that flowed in the streets ! Who directed the guns against the breasts of the workers ? The Czar, the Grand Dukes, the Ministers, the generals and the rabble of the Court. They are murderers. Death to them ! To arms, comrades, occupy the arsenals, the munition stores and the magazines ! Destroy the police stations and gendarmerie offices. We are out to overturn the Czar's Government and to set up our own. Long live the Revolution ! Long live the Constituent Assembly of People's Representatives ! '

The spirit of revolution was certainly abroad, and Lenin felt that another Congress of the Party was essential to co-ordinate effort and direct energy. The Bolshevik element had by now been considerably strengthened as against the Mensheviks. The latter put many obstacles in the way of another Congress, but at length the Third Congress was brought together in London. Martov and his friends boycotted it, and the discussions were in consequence of a different colour. The groups or branches from which the delegates came had still to meet underground and in conditions of secrecy. They were therefore organised in relatively small committees, consisting mainly of the intelligentsia. Lenin came out strongly with the demand that workers must be brought on to the committees in considerable numbers. ' I would like,' he said, ' to see eight workers on our committees for every two intellectuals.' This proposal was strongly opposed and indeed rejected by the majority of the delegates on the grounds that their contacts with the workers were sufficiently close, and that the presence of workers on the committees made conditions of secrecy more difficult.

The question of the Party's policy in relation to the peasants and the land question was also raised and given a much more revolutionary trend than had been expressed in the original programme.

It was now October 1905. Events had marched forward very rapidly in Russia. In October a general strike had been a complete success. The Government appeared to give in, and Count Witte, who had some standing among the Liberal sections, was called back to office by the Czar, who announced that a parliament (Duma) would be set up which, while without power to initiate legislation, would have the right to veto legislation proposed by the Government. This promise tended to conciliate the merchants, business men and middle-class intellectuals.

Lenin now felt that the circumstances called for his return to Russia, and that he would be able safely to do his work there. He travelled back via Stockholm, delayed somewhat on the way, and reached St. Petersburg in early November. This was his first visit since 1900, when he left for Munich, and in the interval he had become the accepted leader of the Bolshevik wing of the Social Democratic Party.

X

THE return to Russia in the conditions prevailing was a great tonic to its future ruler.
True, he had to enter secretly by the back door,
but he could feel in the atmosphere some faint
breaths of a new day. The people had come
out of their cellars ; their voices were heard
in the land ; the mailed fist of the Czar was
palsied by the threatening attitude taken up
by the workers. Even the soldiers and the
sailors showed indications of disloyalty which
were very disquieting to an authority that now
could depend only on force, having no roots in
any great class. The moral authority which
had lasted through the centuries and lived on
the tradition of ' The Little Father ' had been
washed away by the blood of the men and
women who fell before the rifles of the soldiers
in front of the Winter Palace. The defeats in
the war with Japan had deprived Nicholas of
the power to stand before his people as the
great conqueror who expanded the bounds of
his Empire. These were new conditions to

Lenin, who since his brother died in 1887 had felt the power of the Czars pursuing him wherever he might be : as student in Kazan, as prisoner in a fortress in St. Petersburg, among Siberian snows or exile in Munich, London, and Geneva. He decided that he could now live openly in St. Petersburg, and went through the process of registering to make his presence legal. He and his wife took up residence with friends, but they soon found their home surrounded by police spies. Their host produced a revolver and proposed to meet police interference with arms. ' Oh, devil take him,' said Lenin, ' his imprudence will get us into an unnecessary scrape.' The couple decided that to secure freedom of action, it was better to separate and resume their illegal status.

The opportunity for work now was on a different plane both as regards scale and method to what it had been. Maxim Gorky and his wife were jointly responsible for the publication of a legal daily newspaper called *Novaya Zhizn* (New Life). The contributors included both Bolsheviks and Mensheviks. Lenin immediately became a contributor, and his first article took such a clear and pronounced revolutionary line that the more moderate element withdrew, and the paper became to all intents and purposes the official organ of Bolshevism.

The main purpose of his writing at this time was to get his supporters to adapt themselves to the new conditions and to take the fullest advantage of the opportunities of work in the open, particularly in regard to bringing workers into the movement. The older members of his party had become accustomed to the conspiratorial method of work, were loth to depart from it and were inclined to oppose the opening of the narrow party door to new recruits. Lenin relied on the correct Socialist instincts of the workers as the safeguard against the dangers his comrades feared in this wider field of operations.

The other direction of his journalistic effort was towards getting a proper formulation of the relationship between the peasant population and the industrial workers. The general attitude in Socialist circles to this question was that all that was necessary was to throw the peasants some promise of reform in their condition, a sort of ' three acres and a cow ' bribe to secure their more or less passive support for the Socialist policies which the industrial workers were pursuing. Lenin advocated a policy which would make the peasant a conscious revolutionary factor working in co-operation with the workers but by methods appropriate to the economic facts of his life. The consideration of this problem was never far from Lenin's mind. In the earlier *Iskra* days he had written extensively on the state of Russian agriculture and its probable developments. He returned to it again now, in 1905. It played a prominent part in his activity in 1917, and its importance was demonstrated repeatedly in the work of organising the national production in the post-revolutionary period of construction. It can be imagined that he had no easy task to stimulate the interest of his followers in it. Town-dwellers in general and intellectuals in particular find difficulty in sustaining interest in the duller problems of rural life which have an outward appearance of slowness and lack of excitement.

A new instrument had now been forged to aid the forces struggling for Russian freedom. For the first time we hear of the Soviet of Workers' Deputies. How it was called into existence is somewhat obscure, but at its inception there was no idea that it would ultimately become the very corner-stone of the Russian Socialist National structure. Working-class organisation, where it existed, was of the most elementary type. A dispute arising in a particular factory over some special grievance was fought out by organisation improvised for the occasion, with guidance and stimulation from members of the underground Social Democratic circles. Among the concessions made by the Czar in response to the rising spirit of revolt was the setting up of a commission under Shildovsky to examine the grievances of the industrial workers as put forward by delegates chosen by the workers of St. Petersburg. It is possible the Soviet system in its beginnings was brought into existence by the necessity for some machinery for choosing delegates to this commission, and that it then provided the workers of St. Petersburg with their first experience of coming together for consultation. The word ' Soviet,' signifying simply a council, was at its inception as devoid of revolutionary meaning as was the word Bolshevik. In the turmoils of 1905 it speedily assumed importance and became the central repository of working-class power and the forum from which working-class principles and decisions were propounded. Neither the Bolsheviks nor the Mensheviks were responsible for bringing the Workers' Soviet into existence, but Lenin very speedily grasped its essential importance. On one or two occasions he attended its gatherings, a disguised stranger, keeping well out of the gaze of the inquisitive. He gauged its place and function and strongly urged the active participation of his followers in its work. He himself spoke at one session of the St. Petersburg Soviet, on 20th November, on the question of the factory eight-hour day and the lock-out by the employers. Trotsky, although now attached to the Mensheviks, was the most influential of the two hundred delegates who made up the permanent Soviet Assembly, which was at that stage predominantly Menshevik.

Lenin removed to Moscow to follow events there. It also was a seething centre of revolt and discontent, and in much better mood to receive Lenin's propaganda for armed insurrection than St. Petersburg. The latter city had now been the scene of industrial and political struggle for the best part of a year. It had witnessed the Winter Palace massacre. Want and privation were doing their deadly work among the people. Moscow, on the other hand, had as yet experienced much less strenuous conditions ; the people there were ready for a fight, and the Moscow Soviet contained a Bolshevik majority.

The Government watched the spread of revolutionary feeling to other parts of the country than the capital, but sensed the exhaustion from which the people of St. Petersburg were suffering. Although many regiments in the army could not be relied on to support the Czar against the people, and although the navy in the Black Sea was in open revolt, there were still some absolutely loyal guards regiments on which reliance could be placed. The Czarist Government had emerged from the Japanese war burdened with debt, and the feeling of financial insecurity weakened the Czar in any plans for crushing the rebellion; but Count Witte, now recalled to favour, managed to arrange through French agency a substantial loan on favourable terms. Incidentally France secured the support of Russia at the Algeciras Conference over the question of Morocco as against Germany. With money in his pocket, the Czar felt more sure of himself and more able to assert his authority. Count Witte believed it was now possible to crush the rebellion. He ordered the arrest of Nosar, the President of the St. Petersburg Soviet. The arrest was carried out at the end of November, and when no active reprisals followed, the whole Soviet was

arrested in the early part of December.
Czarist power was re-established so far as the
capital was concerned. Deprived of their
leaders, too exhausted by months of struggle
to throw up new ones, the St. Petersburg
workers returned to at least a nominal allegiance to the Czar and their employers.

At this juncture the Moscow workers took
action. Their Soviet declared a general strike,
which met with a unanimous response. The
soldiers on duty within the city displayed a
friendly attitude to the workers. The Soviet
then issued the order that the strike was to be
converted into an armed rising. Hostilities
began in a somewhat half-hearted way, some
bomb-throwing by the workers, spasmodic rifle
fire from the soldiers. On the third day order
and plan began to appear in the workers' forces.
A band of active workers visited all the rifle
dealers and commandeered their stock. The
railway station was placed under an armed
guard. Troops returning from their foreign
service were met as they alighted from the
trains and their ammunition taken by the
rebels. The soldiers of Moscow made no
serious attempt to prevent these incidents.
Their commanding officer then called for
special troops from the capital. Artillery was

brought to bear on the situation, and shells were fired indiscriminately into the populace. This action set the people really aflame, and while the active fighting was left to the militant workers, they had behind them the backing of the whole civil population. For five days they kept up their battle against the trained soldiers of St. Petersburg, but finally had to admit defeat. The defeat of the Moscow rising, following on the crushing of the St. Petersburg movement, meant the end of the 1905 revolution. So far as the achievement of power went, the workers were back where they were before January 1905, but they had gained tremendously in experience. The Czar and his Minister Stolypin now took their vengeance. A thousand persons were put to death without trial ; seventy thousand people were imprisoned, and the deaths in the various risings reached an estimated total of fourteen thousand. Count Witte in his *Memoirs*, speaking of this period of repression, says : ' I need not say that all those who were arrested in connection with the attempt were immediately hanged.' . . . ' The Government began to execute people right and left at the discretion of the administration. Capital punishment, in fact, has become an act of assassination by the

Governmental authorities. Men and women, adult and mere youngsters, are executed alike for a political assassination and for robbing a vodka shop of five roubles.' The Russian people had learned a lesson—in fact several lessons. It may be truly said that the overwhelming mass of Russians never forgave the Czar, nor forgot the part he played both in provoking the revolt and in crushing it.

XI

LENIN did not regard the defeat of 1905 as final.
He believed that a very short period for re-
cuperation would be required to renew the
morale of the workers, and that their fighting
spirit would soon reassert itself. This period,
he thought, would be used by himself and other
responsible leaders in assimilating thoroughly
the lessons to be drawn from the recent events
and in making preparations for the next
attempt. ' We must,' he said, ' more definitely,
practically get down to the tremendous tasks
of a new active movement, preparing for it
more tenaciously, more systematically, more
persistently ; sparing in the greatest degree
possible the forces of the proletariat, worn out
by the strike struggle.' In the meantime it
was necessary for the Bolsheviks to resume
again their old underground methods. Their
daily newspaper, *Novaya Zhizn*, had been closed
down with several others about the same date
as the St. Petersburg Soviet had been arrested,
but Lenin himself still remained in St. Peters-

burg and moved around addressing secret meetings among his followers. The police, however, became too hot on his trail, and at last he had to make his escape out of the country. He crossed the border into Finland, where, being within easy reach of St. Petersburg, he was able to maintain contact with his supporters ; and when preparations were set on foot for a Party Congress to be held at Stockholm he went into St. Petersburg to take part in the preliminary discussions.

The Congress was a full Party one, both Bolsheviks and Mensheviks taking part in it. Two important decisions were taken, first, to launch another newspaper, the *Volna* (The Wave), to take the place of the suppressed *Novaya Zhizn* ; and secondly, that members of the Party should take part in future elections to the Duma, in spite of their deep dissatisfaction with its electoral basis and its very limited powers, and their earlier attitude of boycotting it. The Duma was the first representative parliamentary institution granted to Russia by the Czar. It had been promised in 1905, but the first elections only took place in March 1906.

After the Congress Lenin returned to St. Petersburg, and for the first time spoke in public

in that city at a huge mass meeting on the
9th May. The enthusiasm of the audience
was extraordinary, and although his hopes of
a speedy rising of the revolutionary tide were
vanishing, he must have realised that the forces
were still there ready once more to be called
into action when circumstances were suitable.

In the course of three months the authorities
suppressed in succession two other papers, the
Vpered and *Ekho*, each started to fill the place
of its predecessor. On the 8th July the First
Duma, which had met on the 27th April, was
dissolved, having achieved nothing. There had
been no Social Democrats at the elections ;
the Liberals, or Cadets, as they were called,
had the majority, and there were 150 peasant
representatives who formed a Labour Group.
The constitutionalists during the revolutionary
period had placed their hopes on the Duma ;
indeed, the promise of it had been sufficient
to induce them to withdraw their support from
the workers' strike movement which had forced
the concession of the Duma. The dismissed
Deputies, on discovering their impotence and
resenting their ignominious dismissal, met at
Viborg in Finland and called upon the people
by proclamation to refuse to pay taxes and to
resist recruitment to the army by way of protest.

The call, however, met with no response. While the Duma had been in session Lenin had been writing many articles dealing with the personnel of its members and with the peasant problem. He attacked the Cadet Party hotly, but his articles on the Peasant Group were aimed at arousing them to the need to ally themselves with the workers. He addressed more meetings during this period than he had done at any previous time.

While the call for resistance to tax payment failed as an instrument of protest against the dissolution of the Duma, the Government did not escape difficulties. It followed the dissolution with arrests and repression. Rebellions broke out in Kronstadt and Sveaborg, but these were soon crushed, and the more or less open activity of the Social Democrats had to be abandoned. Underground circle methods had to be resumed once more, and the newest newspaper, *Proletarii*, had to be published illegally.

Lenin had once more to move across the border. He went to stay with friends at Kuokalla in Finland, and their home became for a time the real headquarters of the Bolsheviks. Krupskaya continued working in St. Petersburg, but travelled back and forward from Kuokalla each day. The owners of the house they occupied left shortly after their coming, and Lenin's sister and Krupskaya's mother came to join the family party. Some others of the Bolsheviks who were in danger also took up permanent residence with them, and there was always an open door, either for messengers or refugees. Krupskaya relates : ' The door was never bolted ; a jug of milk and loaf of bread were left in the dining-room over night, and bedding spread on the divan, so that in the event of any one coming on the night train, they could enter without waking anybody, have some refreshment and lie down to sleep. In the morning we often found comrades in the dining-room who had come in the night.' From here Lenin took part in the production of the *Proletarii*, and stimulated his followers to renewed activity (although much in need of stimulation himself). He realised by now that the revolutionary drive of the workers had spent itself and that considerable time would elapse before another similar situation would arrive. His health began to fail, and his ever-watchful wife packed him off into the country with some friends, where he would be clear of the constant stream of visitors who invaded Kuokalla with their daily problems. When he first arrived at this resting-place, Stirsuden, he could not keep himself awake and dozed at all hours of the day. The children of the house called him ' old Drowsy.' When Krupskaya arrived the pair rode about the countryside on old bicycles. The tyres were frequently punctured and were mended with pieces of old goloshes. The holiday soon restored his health, and he got back into harness once more.

He was now so convinced that a revolutionary rising was impossible for some time to come that he strongly urged upon his Bolshevik followers that they should abandon the boycott of the Duma and take an active part in the elections to the Third Duma. As the electoral basis for the Third Duma was even worse than it had been for the previous two, and since its impotence, which he had prophesied, had been then fully demonstrated, he had a considerable task to persuade his followers that an alteration in their tactics was desirable. The ability to make a tactical change when necessary was one of Lenin's strongest characteristics. It proved a most powerful safeguard in his period of greatest responsibility. As soon as he believed that a new tactic was necessary to meet changed conditions, he made the change, even when he had to oppose his most loyal supporters to persuade them of the necessity, and when his later attitude seemed a direct contradiction of his first.

The police search for him in Finland became very intense. This time his capture would have meant certain death. With regret he agreed to return to Switzerland once more. The second going was a more bitter experience than the first. When he first had to leave Russia he was a youth, and knew that a long period of grinding work was needed to create the movement necessary to his purposes ; but now his hopes had been raised high by the 1905 rebellion, and he felt that to leave the scene of action was to accept postponement of his hopes of revolution for a long time ; and he accepted his defeat with bitterness. He set off to Stockholm and waited there till his wife was able to join him. When they left for Switzerland there was a large company of departing Socialists of all parties on the same boat, evidence that Lenin's conclusions about the revolutionary possibilities were pretty general. On their way through Germany they stayed a day or two at Berlin while Lenin renewed acquaintance with Rosa Luxemburg. They reached Geneva on the 20th January 1908. It wore an unwelcome appearance to them as compared with the place they had left with such high hopes two years before.

During these two years he had made his first appearance at an International Socialist Conference. The idea of International co-operation between the working-class movements in various countries had been propounded long before a working-class movement existed at all in many of the countries. The first attempt to carry out the idea was made in September 1864, when the International Working Men's Association was founded in London by leaders of the workers living there. It adopted as its principles a statement written by Karl Marx entitled 'An Address to the Working Classes,' in preference to proposals put forward by the followers of Owen and others proposed by the disciples of Mazzini. This body held successive conferences in London 1865, in Geneva 1866, Lausanne 1867, Brussels 1868, Berne 1869, and the Hague in 1872. The Hague Conference was the last of this particular series of international gatherings. After a lapse of several years there was a revival in 1889, when a Congress was held in Paris. There were in fact two Congresses, one an attempt to revive the previous series, and another, emanating from

Germany, which was avowedly Socialist and Marxist. From this time onwards International Socialist Congresses were held regularly at intervals of three years, while a smaller body called the International Socialist Bureau met at more frequent intervals. They had a permanent headquarters, first at Brussels, for a short time in London, and latterly at Zurich. These two international efforts came to be known in the working-class movement by the short titles of First International and Second International. The Stuttgart Conference of the Second International was Lenin's first experience of conference with the organised workers of other lands. He had met several of the leading personalities previously, and had watched the activities of the German and British movements as an onlooker. He attended subsequently other conferences of the Second International. He was not impressed with it from the start, and finally, through its failure at the outbreak of the war, he came to mistrust it completely. When he achieved power in Russia, one of the first tasks he undertook was to form a new International, the Third.

XII

LENIN had formed a warm friendship with Maxim Gorky, and shortly after his return to Geneva received an invitation to visit Gorky in the island of Capri where he was living, an invitation he wished very much to accept. He wrote : ' Your letter gave me great pleasure. It would be fine to come to Capri. I will certainly get free some time and visit you. . . . When,' he adds, ' is the weather quite particularly nice at Capri ? ' At that time, however, he was unable to pay the promised visit, for besides being immersed in work on a fresh newspaper project, and lacking money for the journey, he was very much preoccupied over a philosophic dispute that had arisen within the Party. This dispute concerned the new philosophy called by the high-sounding title of Empirio-Criticism. To the general reader of philosophic books it did not appear to be a particularly pernicious brand of philosophy, but to Lenin's critical mind it contained all the elements of a religion, a denial of materialism on which his Marxist faith was built, and

tendencies which would take the minds of
Socialists away from practical realities into the
realm of vague and idealistic aspirations. He
saw real danger in its acceptance by his friends
and followers, and set himself with his characteristic thoroughness to its study, in order
that he might combat its influence in the Party.
To do so, he had to range himself against men
who had been his firm supporters in previous
controversies, and against men who had the
reputation of being deep students of philosophy,
a reputation which Lenin did not possess.
Amongst those who had taken up the new
philosophy with great enthusiasm were Bogdanov and Lunarcharsky, while Gorky was also
somewhat affected by it. Lenin went into the
subject very thoroughly, even paying a visit to
London in order to avail himself of the material
in the library of the British Museum. The
result of his researches was embodied in a series
of letters to friends, articles in the Party paper,
and an imposing volume entitled *Materialism
and Empirio-Criticism*. He may or may not have
had a philosophic mind—opinion on that must
depend on one's definition of that somewhat
indefinite entity—but certainly in this work
he handled his material in the fashion of the
masters. The following quotation is a perfect

example of the classic form of philosophical controversy : ' Beyond the epistemological scholasticism of empirio-criticism it is impossible not to discern clearly the partisan struggle in philosophy, a struggle which ultimately expresses the tendencies and ideology of classes hostile to one another in modern society. Recent philosophy is as partisan as it was two thousand years ago. The contending parties are in the main materialism and idealism, although their nature may be concealed under a pseudo-erudite phraseological charlatanry or beneath the guise of a stupid non-partisanship.' While in form classical, the content of the above quotation is a strong reaffirmation of the class struggle and the materialistic conception of history as being the only sound basis upon which a Socialist could found his thinking.

The leaders of the Empirio-Criticist philosophic school among the Social Democrats regarded themselves as propounding the very latest thing in philosophy, something which represented an advance on all previous philosophies. They believed that Lenin in his opposition to it was out of date, and that his political deviations, such as his advocacy of participation in the work of the Duma, was evidence of it. It must have been irksome to them to read his merciless analysis of their up-to-date revolutionary philosophy, which he traced back to its source in Bishop Berkeley, English Churchman and philosopher of eighteenth-century bourgeois England. He quotes Berkeley as saying : ' Our knowledge of these hath been very much obscured and confounded and we have been led into very dangerous errors by supposing a twofold existence of the objects of the sense—the one intelligible or in the mind, the other real and without the mind.' And Berkeley ridicules such absurd notions which admit the possibility of thinking the unthinkable ! The source of the absurdity ' follows from our supposing a difference between things and ideas—and depends on the supposition of external objects.' The same source—discovered in Berkeley in 1710 and again by Bogdanov in 1908—produces faith in fetiches and idols : ' The existence of matter or bodies unperceived has not only been the main support of Atheists and Fatalists, but on the same principle doth Idolatry likewise in all its various forms depend.'

Lenin was annoyed that he should be obliged to spend time and effort which he could ill spare from his real work, in attempting to drive out of the minds of Socialists foolish anti-

Marxist ideas which he felt they should have known better than to entertain. Writing to Gorky in March 1908, he says : ' I am neglecting the paper on account of my passion for philosophy. To-day I am studying an empiriocriticist and swearing like a trooper. To-morrow I shall read another and curse like a bargee. And Innokentii rightly blames me for neglecting the *Proletarii*. Things will not go right.'

In April Gorky suggested a meeting to bridge the gulf between the disputants, but Lenin replied that ' It would be useless, even harmful for me to come. I cannot and will not deal with people whose aim is to advocate a union of scientific socialism with religion. It is absurd to dispute and useless to wear down one's nerves. Philosophy must be kept separate from Party affairs. . . . If A wants to attack B, or B A, on account of his philosophical views, that must be done separately, that is, without harm to the Cause.'

The dispute reached such proportions that rival schools were set up to educate Party members in the principles of the contending views. The Empirio-Criticists had their school at Capri and later at Bologna, while Lenin's school was at Longjumeau, near Paris, to which place he had moved from Geneva.

Fortunately the antagonism between the two groups did not leave the same deep resentment as had the disputes on tactics, and the rival leaders still continued to work together in the Party.

Meantime, while Lenin was engaged in philosophical controversy, events were moving in Russia. In the period of reaction Count Stolypin had succeeded Witte as the Czar's chief Minister. When the Czar was faced with military defeat, financial difficulties and a hostile people, he was glad of the services of Witte (who had Liberal tendencies and definite ideas about the development of Russia) to help him out of his troubles ; but Stolypin was a man more after his own heart, and he turned to him to carry out the repressive measures that the return to a normal state of affairs in the country made possible. | Stolypin was assassinated at the end of 1910, but before his death he had introduced a new land policy, over the heads of the Duma, with the object of breaking up the Mir (the traditional land commune) and allowing the development of a class of independent farmers working on a fairly large scale—the Kulak class, which became a source of great difficulty to the Revolutionary Government in after years. Economically, the country was being developed with considerable rapidity, and the economic developments were producing changes in the social structure of the community ; but the political attitude of the new classes tended to follow the usual lines ; that is, the old nobility and the big landlords were Conservative in outlook and supported the Czarist régime, while the new capitalists, commercial men and intellectuals, were Liberal, belonging to the Party of Constitutional Democrats popularly known as Cadets, and the large mass of the workers gave their adherence to one or other section of the Socialist Movement.

An attempt to achieve unity between the two sections of the Social Democratic Party was made at a Congress held in Paris, but failed completely. The final break did not come till January 1912, when Lenin summoned a special Congress at Prague, at which the Bolsheviks definitely severed their connection with the Mensheviks. This year, 1912, was one of importance to the Russian working-class movement. In April two hundred strikers in the Lena goldfields were shot down by the police, with the result that industrial and social discontent spread like wildfire among the workers, and strikes broke out in every part of the country until no section was left out of the struggle. Although Lenin had come round to the view that the Socialists ought to take part in the elections and the work of the Duma, he never regarded parliamentary action as being of primary importance, and he welcomed the outbreak of industrial unrest as the opening of a new era of revolutionary activity. Stimulated as always by the atmosphere of industrial struggle, he set to work to meet the new spirit by the production of a purely Bolshevik daily paper, called *Pravda* (Truth), which thereafter came out daily in St. Petersburg, and became very popular with the industrial workers among whom it was secretly distributed. From his place of exile Lenin contributed a daily article to it and controlled its policy, but he felt that Paris was too far away from the scene of action. Once more he moved his camp to settle at Poronin, near Cracow in Galicia, so near to Russia that an ordinary walk brought him to the frontier. In the Fourth Duma, elected this year, six Bolshevik Deputies were returned, and formed a little independent Party, which was now able to work under his direct control. His life at Poronin was much like what it had been at Kuokalla. He was in close daily contact with people from the scene of action, instead of being surrounded only with Russian exiles like himself. He was able to measure for himself the progress of his newspaper and keep in close touch with all the branches of revolutionary activity, press, parliament and general organisation. In this way he kept them all steadily directed towards the one end of hammering into the minds of the workers the idea that liberty could only be obtained by the forcible overthrow of the Czarist régime. One big disappointment came to him in the discovery that Malinowsky, the leader of the Parliamentary Party, was a police agent. Lenin had liked him and placed great trust in him, and for long refused to believe the rumours of his treachery. The evidence finally became undeniable, and Malinowsky, feeling exposure imminent, himself confirmed it by taking refuge in flight. In spite of this set-back the work went on steadily; faith was too strong and hopes too high to permit of one Judas destroying the cause.

Towards the end of July 1914, the rumour of war spread throughout Europe, and in the early days of August the troops began to march to the frontiers. In Paris, Jaurés, the French Socialist leader and a prominent member of the Socialist International, was assassinated. Socialists in European countries called meetings to protest against war, but before their meetings assembled war was already a grim reality.

XIII

THE outbreak of war was an appalling calamity for the peoples of Europe. It was a personal calamity for Lenin as well. He waited, expecting that the Socialists of Europe, in particular the powerful Social Democrats of Germany, would raise effective protest. When the news came that the Socialists of Germany, with the exception of Karl Liebknecht, had voted the war credits, he at first refused to believe. Soon he learnt that the French Socialists, the Belgian Socialists, the Russian Mensheviks and the British Labour Party (with the exception of the Independent Labour Party) had all fallen in behind their governments in support of the war, and that the Second International, of which he was a member, which had passed high-sounding resolutions expressing its opposition to war and its intention to prevent it at Stuttgart in 1906, had collapsed in the presence of war itself. Lenin, though perhaps he had not expected very much from the International in the way of opposition to war, was not pre-

pared for such a complete collapse. Now that
he saw his comrades of Stuttgart joining their
capitalist governments for the purpose of the
energetic prosecution of the war, he wrote off
the Second International as a factor making
for Socialism. The Russian workers also, in
whom he had placed confidence, lined up
behind their Czar—the Czar who had shot
them down in 1905 before the Winter Palace,
who was responsible for shooting them down
in the Lena goldfields. Towards the workers
and the Socialist leaders Lenin felt differently.
The workers, he thought, did not understand ;
they had been taught to believe that men must
fight for their fatherland ; they did not understand that the motives that took their rulers to
war sprang from economic interests which were
not the interests of the mass of the people, and
they had no vision of the world Socialist Commonwealth. But the members of the Second
International did know, or ought to have
known, and had, or should have had the vision.
While the people were children sinning in
ignorance, the Socialist leaders were sinning
against the light.

Now that the war had started and seemed
likely to last a considerable time, Lenin faced a
new situation. What should a Socialist do in

such circumstances ? Should he cry for peace
where there was no peace ? He settled the
question in his own decisive way ; he must use
the circumstances of war and the difficulties
that it would make for the rulers to encompass
their overthrow by the working class. But he
soon found himself up against difficulties. As
a Russian citizen he was an enemy alien where
he lived in Galicia. The most innocent movements of the alien were cause of suspicion and
sinister interpretation. He was arrested at the
instance of the Austrian Government and
thrown into prison as a Russian spy. His comrades were very much alarmed. If the charge
were proved, and at that time spy charges were
much easier to prove than to disprove, he would
be handed over to the military authorities,
whose way with spies was short and sharp.
The Socialists moved on his behalf, and Victor
Adler, the veteran leader of the Austrian
Socialists, was able to prove to the Austrian
Government from his personal knowledge of
the man, that so far from being an agent of
Russian Czarism, Lenin was a more bitter
enemy of the Czar than any one in Austria.
On these representations he was soon released,
and after some delay was permitted to remove
into Switzerland. In his Austrian prison his

only opportunities for political activity were among his fellow-prisoners, which opportunities he used to the full, but in the neutral atmosphere of Switzerland he found more scope, though the war conditions of the surrounding countries made limitations even here. He produced pamphlets analysing the causes of the war and laying down his view of a correct Socialist policy in war conditions. The subject-matter of these pamphlets was laid before the group of Russian Socialists then in exile in Berne, and also sent by means of the usual devices into Russia, where the Duma Group adopted them as the basis of its parliamentary policy. It can easily be imagined that it was a difficult task to enunciate during a war a policy which called upon the people to work for the defeat of their own armies, which asked for the transformation of the war into a civil war, and which based itself on the view that the war was not one for liberty, justice or any other moral end, but was solely for the selfish ends of capitalist imperialism. The Duma Group did not shirk the task, and they speedily met the consequences. They were arrested and condemned to penal servitude in Siberia. When men go to prison for a principle their imprisonment itself makes propaganda for that principle. So it was in this case, and their imprisonment, together with the growing realisation of the real meaning of war, soon began to destroy its early glamour. In the beginning of a war, martial glory, a spurious patriotism, hold men's minds, but later on the glory becomes faded, the patriotism less urgent ; death strikes into the homes of the people ; mutilated men appear in the streets, poverty and privation become more pronounced, and men begin to ponder the why and the wherefore of the war, and finding its justification difficult, go on to ask the question, ' Who is to blame ? ' In Russia that question was easily answered. It is one of the defects of absolute monarchy from the monarch's point of view that while in the days of triumph he monopolises the glory, in days of defeat, discontent and despair he has a monopoly of the blame. Czar Nicholas had a double dose of unpopularity in the period of war weariness ; his past rose up to haunt him ; the Winter Palace could not be forgotten ; the Czaritza was believed to be against the Allies, while the evil influence of the powerful and hated Rasputin added greatly to his unpopularity.

Lenin's chief thought was for the revolutionary possibilities in Russia, but he was not forgetful of the rest of the world, and when the Italian Socialists convened a Conference at Zimmerwald of Socialists from the different countries who wanted immediate peace, he attended it. As was natural in the circumstances, most of those present were pacifists. These pacifists who desired only the end of the war were not the perfect allies of Lenin, who wanted the war ended by the outbreak of revolution in each of the warring countries ; but he found some kindred souls who formed a group with him, and when a further Conference came together at Kienthal near Berne in 1916, there was a substantial backing for his attitude. Lenin was a perfervid believer in the necessity for international Socialist action, but his experience of the Socialist International, both before and during the war, had brought him to the conclusion that it was a useless instrument from the Socialist point of view, and that a new International must be formed. His historical survey of the International was presented in the form of an extended resolution at the All-Russian Conference of the Russian Social Democratic Party held 7th to 12th May 1917, after his return to Russia. The Third International and its activities have been the subject of controversy in every country in the

world, and part of the resolution is worth
quoting in detail on that account.

' In most of the European workers' Parties
opportunism gained the upper hand before
the beginning of the present war. With the
beginning of the imperialist war in 1914
opportunism turned into social-chauvinism,
into "defencism." The defencists proclaimed "national defence" in the predatory
imperialist war and perpetrated a betrayal
of the cause of the working class. Opportunism caused the collapse of the Second
International.

' During the war three main tendencies
were developed inside the world labour
movement :—

' (1) The defencists of all countries broke
with Socialism ; they became a tool of their
respective imperialist governments to pro-
long the war ; in practice they became class
enemies of the proletariat.

' (2) The "centre" whose main leaders
are Kautsky and Haase in Germany, Longuet
and Pressemane in France, Axelrod and
others in Russia, Robert Grimm in Switzerland, Turati and others in Italy, have sub-
stituted pacifism for revolutionary socialism.
The "centre" does not call upon the
workers to overthrow the capitalist governments, but it tries to persuade the present

imperialist governments to conclude a democratic peace. Vacillating as it does between internationalism and defencism, not advocating in war-time a revolutionary struggle against their governments, the " centre " insists on unity with the defencists on an international scale, without drawing the necessary conclusions from the split that occurred in the Social Democratic parties, a split that has taken place even in a country like Germany.

' (3) There are the revolutionary internationalists who have started a struggle against the war in all countries in spite of martial law and an iron-clad régime. Such are the groups of Karl Liebknecht and that of the Arbeiterpolitik in Germany ; John McLean, Tom Mann, the Left Wing of the British Socialist Party, and the Independent Labour Party in England ; Loriot and his comrades in France : the Left Wing of the Socialist Party in Italy ; the comrades grouped around the Viennese Karl Marx Club in Austria ; the Socialist Labour Party and the group publishing the periodical " Internationalist " in the United States of America; the party that has broken with the defencists and which is led by Comrade Höglund and others in Sweden ; the Tribunist Party in Holland ; the comrades grouped around the periodical "Youth International" in Switzerland. The tendency that is at the present moment represented by the above-named groups has started a struggle against the capitalists of the respective countries during and in spite of the war, it has broken with the respective "defencists," and it has started a struggle against the "centre." This is the only tendency that has remained loyal to Socialism. The Socialist future belongs to this tendency alone.

' The majority in Zimmerwald and Kienthal belonged to the centre. This weakened the Zimmerwald bloc from the very start. The Zimmerwald bloc as a whole rejected the proposal made by its Left section relative to calling the workers of all countries to an immediate revolutionary struggle against their governments. The Zimmerwald bloc refused to recognise the necessity of a straight split with the social-chauvinists' majority of the old official parties, and thus it weakened the Zimmerwald movement. . . . The task of our party, operating as it does in a country where the revolution started earlier than in other countries, is to take the initiative of creating the Third International which is finally to break with "defencism" and to wage a decisive struggle against the middle-of-the-road policy of the "centre" as well.'

The double interest in this statement is first in its demonstration of Lenin's detailed knowledge of the groups and leading individuals in the various countries whose point of view was similar to his own, and also of those whom he regarded as his antagonists, and secondly, in its repetition by him in international affairs of the same point of view as produced the controversy that led to the split between the Bolshevik and Menshevik sections in the Russian Socialist Party. Only those who had proved themselves were entitled to admission to the order, and to him the attitude to the war was a test question.

In Switzerland, where he was living in the latter part of the year 1916, his personal life followed the same simple course as always, except that this natural Spartan simplicity had perforce to be still more simple owing to his more straitened circumstances. The ordinary machinery of the Party in Russia had been reduced to a bare skeleton as a result of war restrictions, and the Party finances had gone to vanishing point. The total membership of the Party at this period was not more than 20,000, scattered in small groups in all parts of Russia, and in emigrant groups in different countries abroad. This was a big advance on the membership in 1905, which did not reach

10,000. The great access of membership to the Bolsheviks came in the few months after the Kerensky Revolution, when the Party increased its numbers between February and August from 23,000 to 200,000. The meagre pittance that constituted his income from Party funds in times of relative prosperity diminished in proportion to the Party's difficulties. He continued his studies with the highest concentration, wrote some of his most important works, notably *Imperialism as the Latest Stage of Capitalism*, and talked to whatever sympathetic groups he could gather around him.

Meantime war weariness at home in Russia, the stories trickling back from the front to Moscow and St. Petersburg of the evil plight of the soldiers, the privations of the civilian population, the pressure of Russia's Allies for a more energetic prosecution of the war, all carried on his agitation for him in Russia while he worked on the theory and practice of revolution away in Zurich.

XIV

At length the day arrived for which Lenin
waited. The revolutionary wave was sweeping
up. The Liberal section in the Duma were
anxious to improve the war organisation of
Russia, and a great campaign to increase the
production of munitions was started in St.
Petersburg and Moscow, while efforts were
made to rouse the 'will to victory.' The
workers, however, under the influence of Lenin's
teaching, did not play up. Instead, on the
3rd of March 1917, a strike broke out in the
Putilov Metal Works in St. Petersburg, which a
week later developed into a general strike
throughout the city. The Soviet of Workers'
Deputies sprang into life again, and within a
few days the soldiers began to come over to the
side of the workers. Then Moscow joined in.
In the 1905 Revolution Moscow's effort came
nearly a year after that of St. Petersburg. In
March 1917 there was no delay. Ten days
after the strike movement started in St. Petersburg a general strike took place in Moscow,

and there also the Soviet of Workers' Deputies came to life.

Meantime, Rasputin had been murdered; but while his evil influence was out of the way, the evil reputation of the Czar remained. All sympathy and support departed from him almost overnight; he was blamed for all the troubles. Feeling that his time was come, he abdicated in favour of his brother, the Grand Duke Michael; but things had gone too far for any Romanov to attempt to rule Russia, and Michael's reign ended within twenty-four hours. He also took the better course and abdicated. With the passing of the Czar authority fell into the hands of the Duma, which for purposes of government acted through an Executive Committee.

Two days after the abdication of the Czar the issue of *Pravda* was resumed, and Lenin's voice rang once more through the land. On 18th March, simultaneously with the appearance of *Pravda*, the Soviet called off the strike. On 16th March Lenin wrote from Switzerland to his comrade Madame Kollontai, also in exile : ' The workers have been fighting in bloody battles for a week, yet Miliukov plus Guchkov plus Kerensky are in power. The same old European pattern. . . . Well, what of it ! This first stage of the first revolution will be neither final nor confined to Russia. We, of course, retain our opposition to the defence of the fatherland, to the imperialist slaughter directed by Shingavev plus the Kerenskys and Co. . . . We shall see how the People's Freedom Party (which commands a majority in the new Cabinet, Konovalov being inclined rather " to the Left," while Kerensky is decidedly more to the Left !) will give the people freedom, bread and peace. . . . We shall see ! '

The first big blow had been struck in the accomplishment of the task that Lenin had declared inevitable. Sometimes he had been almost alone in his faith, but that faith never wavered as he steadily worked to fit himself and the workers for the part he and they had to play. The day had arrived, and he was in exile. Trotsky, who had been separated from him for many years, both by Party differences and by the Atlantic Ocean, was also in exile, and learnt the news of the Revolution from the American papers in a Canadian concentration camp. The call to the scene of action was not to be resisted ; Lenin was at once all on edge to return to Russia, but to return was not easy. He had to pass through the territory of one or other of the belligerent countries, and he was not *persona grata* with the Allied Governments. Speed was to him the paramount consideration. After rejecting the idea of acquiring a Swedish passport and travelling as a Swede, and considering all sorts of impossible ways of getting through, he approached his Swiss Socialist friends, Robert Grimm and Fritz Platten, to negotiate a passage for him through Germany. Though he knew that this would be likely to rouse the suspicion that he was pro-German, he decided to take the risk, while using every possible precaution to safeguard his reputation from such a charge. He also took the precaution of stating in full in *Pravda* on 18th May the conditions on which he and his fellow-Socialists were permitted to travel through Germany. He arrived at St. Petersburg on 16th April. His old comrade Plekhanov beat him on the return journey by three days. Trotsky was a little later.

When Lenin arrived at the station, dressed in somewhat threadbare clothes, he was received with acclamation. On his former visits to St. Petersburg his comrades and disciples had never dared to show themselves for fear of calling the attention of the police to him and to themselves, so that he was unprepared for the great reception awaiting him. He stepped from his carriage armed, not with revolver or bombs, but with a thesis, which proved something in the nature of a bomb to his comrades, for they were in a mood of exultation over the recent achievements, while his mind was addressing itself to what had still to be done. They would have been glad to continue the jubilations ; he had to examine the situation in all its aspects and to decide on the next steps.

The thesis opened with the sentence : ' In our attitude toward the war not the slightest concession must be made to " revolutionary defencism," for under the new government of Lvov and Co., owing to the capitalist nature of this government, the war on Russia's part remains a predatory imperialist war.' This part of the thesis ended with the words, ' This view is to be widely propagated among the army units in the field,' and he urged also the necessity of making it clear to the mass of the people. Not only was this policy something of a shock to his Bolshevik comrades ; it was also very distasteful to the Provisional Government newly set up. They were still at the stage of wondering what to do next, and the one thing clear in their minds was that they had to continue the war until such time as the Allies were ready unitedly to conclude peace.

Lenin had, in fact, few supporters among political leaders for the immediate termination of the war. It was easy to misrepresent him as a pro-German; both his release from Austria in the early months of the war and his free passage through Germany on his return home could be used as evidence against him by those who wished. Fortunately he had foreseen that possibility, and taken the precaution, already referred to, of having his negotiations in each case carried through by persons of standing in the Socialist movement. In the latter case he could point to well-witnessed documents to show that he had made no bargain with Germany beyond promising to try to secure the exchange of an equal number of German prisoners from Russia for the Socialists allowed to pass through. While political people, including some of the leading men among the Bolsheviks, were all opposed to his policy, it expressed the clear desires of both workers and soldiers.

On the evening after his arrival he spoke at length to a meeting of the caucus of the Bolshevik Party. He urged that the Soviet must cease to regard itself as an organisation for exerting pressure on the Government. It must think of itself as the Government. ' The art of government,' he said, ' cannot be gotten out of books. Try, make mistakes, learn how to govern.' These were other items in the programme which he asked his supporters to accept : ' Confiscation of all private lands ; immediate merger of all the banks in the country into one general national bank ; immediate placing of the Soviet of Workers' Deputies in control of social production and distribution of goods.' His colleague of former times could not swallow such a programme. In *Pravda* of 20th April Lenin referred to Plekhanov's criticism of it : ' In his paper Mr. Plekhanov called my speech " delirious." Very good, Mr. Plekhanov. But how awkward, uncouth and slow-witted you are in your polemics ! If I talked delirious stuff for two whole hours, why did an audience of hundreds tolerate this delirium ? Further, why does your paper devote a whole column to reproducing this delirium ? You have indeed made a bad shot in this matter ! It is, of course, much easier to shout, to scold, to rave, than to make an attempt to relate, to explain, to recall how Marx and Engels, in 1871, 1872 and 1875, viewed the experience of the Paris Commune, and the kind of state the proletariat needs. The former Marxist, Mr. Plekhanov, probably does not wish to think about Marxism.'

As in former days, his first real battle was with his own Bolshevik supporters. In accordance with his theory, it was necessary that they should fully understand the position and view it clearly in the light of Marxist principles. Writing in *Pravda* on 28th April, he says : ' The basic question in any revolution is that of state power. Unless this is understood, there can be no intelligent participation in the revolution, let alone direction of it. What has made our revolution so strikingly unique is that it has established dual power. This fact must be grasped first. Unless it be understood, there can be no further advance. . . . What constitutes dual power ? The fact that by the side of the Provisional Government, the government of the bourgeoisie, there has developed another, as yet weak, embryonic, but undoubtedly real and growing government—the Soviet of Workers' and Soldiers' Deputies.' He returned to this theme again and again, to drive home to his comrades the fact that the Revolution was so far only half a revolution ; that the further stages were not to be accomplished by establishing the existing Provisional Government, bourgeois in form and origin, into a permanent government, democratically elected on the parliamentary model ; but that they must carry out their revolutionary duty by developing the Soviet power to the point where it could become the Provisional Government. In the conditions it was a difficult task he set himself. The precedents in other countries among Socialist Parties were to take the parliamentary machine if there were one, or to advocate the establishment of a parliament if none existed, and to work towards securing a Socialist majority. Lenin looked for the best instrument available of working-class creation and representation, found it in the Soviets, and saw in them the beginnings of the future constitution of the Socialist Republic. The nearest precedent he could find in history was in the short-lived Paris Commune. So anxious was he to break with all the bourgeois traditions of the past that he began to make a demand for a change in the Party name, from Socialist to Communist, so that there should be no confusion of his beliefs and those of his Party with the beliefs of those European Socialists who had entered into coalition with their respective Governments for the prosecution of the war.

On his comrades who resisted his innovations

he poured out his invective. To the reasons they advanced for their objections he answered : ' This reason is based solely on laziness, somnolence and love of routine. We want to rebuild the world. We want to end this imperialist World War in which hundreds of millions of people are involved and billions of dollars are invested, a war which cannot be ended in a truly democratic way without the greatest proletarian revolution in history. And here we are, afraid of our own shadow. Here we are keeping on our backs the same old soiled shirt. . . . It is high time to cast off the soiled shirt. It is high time to put on clean linen.' Although Trotsky, much to Lenin's regret, had taken the Menshevik side in the old controversy, he was one of the earliest active converts to Lenin's view now. He threw himself actively into the work alongside Lenin, and while Lenin analysed, explained and demonstrated, Trotsky used all his great oratorical power to sway his comrades and the masses of workers to Lenin's support. Their influence began to make itself felt. A gulf opened between the Provisional Government and the Petrograd Soviet.

The population had maintained a high level of political consciousness ever since the overthrow of the Czar, and when in the early days of May the Danish Socialists were endeavouring to get together a Conference in Stockholm to discuss conditions for concluding peace, the Petrograd Soviet agreed to the proposal. This represented a serious break with the Government, which had issued a Note to the Allies assuring them that the Provisional Government would fully meet its obligations to them, and that the people were behind them in carrying the war to a decisive victory. Instead of acting in the spirit of this Note the people were out on the streets demonstrating against Miliukov, the Minister responsible for its issue, and were supported by certain of the regiments in the demonstrations.

In face of these evidences of popular disapproval, the Government declared its intention of broadening its basis to include representatives who were presumed to have influence with the discontented workers. Guchkov, Minister of War, and Miliukov, Minister of Education, resigned from the Government, and the Executive of the Petrograd Soviet declared itself in favour of a Coalition Government. On the 18th of May the Coalition Government was formed, and included in the Ministry were representatives of the Mensheviks and the

various Socialist groups to the Right of them.
Prince Lvov was Prime Minister. Tsereteli
and Skobelev of the Mensheviks held the
respective positions of Minister of Posts and
Minister of Labour ; Kerensky and Chernov
of the Socialist-Revolutionists were respec-
tively Minister of War and Minister of Agriculture ; two members of the People's Socialist
Party held the Ministries of Justice and
Supplies.

From its inception Lenin denounced this
combination as useless either for the purpose
of bringing peace or of furthering the progress
of the Revolution. In *Pravda* of 27th May he
attacked the Coalition Government as a
capitalist government, and its Socialist ministers
as tools of capitalism, and warned the people
against trusting it or hoping for anything from it.
On 2nd June he asked, ' Has dual power disappeared ? ' and answered the question in the
negative, but pointed out that the question of
state power was still in an indefinite, unstable
and transitory condition. ' Every one realises
that the country is on the brink of an abyss —
yet all we do about it is engage in bureaucratic
dallying. The root of the error of the Narodniks (or Social Revolutionaries) and the Mensheviks is in their not understanding the class

struggle which they want to displace, disguise, attenuate with phrases, promises, makeshifts, commissions, with the participation of representatives . . . of the same dual government. Dual power is still with us. The government of the capitalists remains a government of the capitalists despite the small addition in a minority capacity of a few Narodniks and Mensheviks. The Soviets remain the organisation of the majority. The Narodnik and Menshevik leaders are helplessly tossing about hither and thither trying to take up a position " on the fence." And the crisis is growing.'

Although the Socialist Ministers received the consent of their respective parties to participate in the Coalition, it became clear that their action was not fully approved when, on 7th June, at the Congress of his Party, Kerensky was defeated for membership of the Central Committee of the Socialist-Revolutionists. As Minister of War he had already ordered preparations for the offensive. Discontent was becoming very pronounced both in the Army and the Navy, and the Bolsheviks published, in addition to *Pravda*, a special newspaper for the soldiers. The dual nature of power in Russia was becoming more evident. A number of regiments were disbanded at the front for refusing to take the offensive. The Prime Minister, Lvov, in tones of deep moral indignation, raged against ' the virtual truce that is being established at the front.' ' Let every worker,' said Lenin, ' think well over those thunderous diatribes against a " virtual truce." Millions of people have been killed and maimed in the war. Unheard-of sufferings have fallen to the lot of the people, particularly the toiling masses, in consequence of the war. While the capitalists are reaping scandalously high profits, the soldiers are being cruelly maimed and tortured. What wrong is there in a " virtual truce " ? What harm is done if the slaughter ceases ? What wrong is there in the soldiers getting a brief respite ? ' Such language as this made its appeal both to the soldiers and the civilian population. Congresses both of workers and of soldiers were assembling, and the issues they discussed were the issues that Lenin was posing to the nation. The most important of all these Congresses, the All-Russian Congress of Soviets of Workers' and Soldiers' Deputies, opened on 16th June, and here again they discussed their problems as they were being stated daily by Lenin. He analysed the situation, formulated the policies, and all the time made the pace. The Navy had fewer opportunities of taking part in the movement on land, but they were not left untouched by the general surging up of political consciousness. On 19th June the sailors arrested their officers at Sebastopol, and a gathering of sailors' delegates demanded the resignation of Admiral Koltchak. Lenin kept his eyes on every move and supported every effort, whether by workers, soldiers or sailors, to express their political will. The peasants had greater difficulty in finding organised expression, but they also held their Congress, and Lenin in his speeches and newspaper articles analysed their problems, enunciated a land policy, and encouraged their organisation, especially among the poorer peasants.

More than at any previous time, Lenin now displayed those habits of systematic intensive study and mental activity which had been so characteristic of him from his boyhood onwards. No aspect of the national life was allowed to escape his critical examination. Nor was his Marxist theory set aside for the duration of the trouble, as being something academic, without application to practical affairs. He insisted on testing every situation in the light of Marx's teaching, and basing every proposal on the principles of the master.

XV

THE months of May, June and July, 1917, gave Lenin the first opportunity he had had in a lifetime of forty-seven years of freely meeting the people of Russia. He made the fullest use of the time. He met them in the mass ; he met them in small groups ; and he met them intimately as individuals. He taught, and he learned. The Bolsheviks had occupied as their headquarters the Palace of Khesinskaia, a former mistress of the Czar, and a well-known ballet dancer. Among other advantages it possessed a balcony in a position that made it an ideal forum for addressing a large audience gathered in front in the open air. Lenin made almost daily use of it to spread his ideas among the people. The prevalent political excitement made it easy to get an audience, and every day events occurred that gave him a new text and new arguments for his main theme, which did not vary, but consisted in the re-iterated exhortation to the workers to seize power and use it.

The Government presented a wide front for attack. Despite the fact that there had been a revolution and a Czar had been deposed, nothing essential was changed. The new Government allowed itself to be simply carried along on the momentum of the old Czarist Government, with the same officials, the same police control, the same economic system, the same war with the same objects. It can easily be imagined that a Government not too sure of itself in any case, felt this steady, unrelenting attack very keenly. The majority of the Government naturally expected that when the Socialist representatives entered the Government, hostile criticism from Socialist quarters would cease. There can be little doubt that the Socialist Ministers did their best to end it. The Press of the Socialist-Revolutionists and of the Mensheviks also attempted to stifle criticism at this juncture, but the voice from the balcony of Khesinskaia's Palace would not be stifled ; the pen that wrote in *Pravda* kept covering paper. Condemnatory resolutions from the Soviet failed to silence them, and then the Government began to think in terms of coercion. A Bolshevik Demonstration was banned, but agitation and propaganda still went on.

The Government now proceeded to show that it was doing things. It announced that the elections for the Constituent Assembly would take place on 30th September, and that it would meet on 13th October. This arrangement left a full three months to elapse, a much longer time than a country with established parliamentary institutions allows, even when there is no special crisis to be met. Two days later, Kerensky issued orders to the Army and Navy to open the new offensive. The conditions laid down by the Petrograd Soviet governing the participation of the Socialist representatives in the Coalition Government included : (1) active work in the interest of peace ; (2) regulation of industry and reform of finance ; (3) preparatory measures for the solution of the agrarian and labour questions ; (4) the speediest convocation of the Constituent Assembly. To issue instructions for a new offensive and an intimation of an election at a date three months distant was a very limited attempt to fulfil the conditions. The new offensive met with a certain degree of success, and an attempt was made to whip up the enthusiasm of the people on the basis of victory for the Army of the Revolution. The Government began to feel itself a little stronger in the saddle. An economic Council was set up to begin to organise the production and distribution of the nation's goods.

The period of triumph and confidence was short-lived. Within a week the advancing army was driven back in circumstances which displayed a complete lack of any desire to fight. Kerensky's chief work for weeks previously had been to tour the front addressing the soldiers to work them up to fighting pitch. The hard facts of battle proved more potent than his oratory. As the army retreated, the temper of the Petrograd workers rose, and an armed demonstration of the workers took place with the approval and support of the soldiers. With things going wrong a scapegoat had to be found. Who would make a better scapegoat than Lenin ? He was the most difficult critic of the Government. His influence with the people was great and growing greater. He must be put out of public life under conditions that would discredit him in the eyes of the people. The cry of pro-German was set around. It was a favourite cry in all the Allied countries between 1914 and 1917 against any one who uttered criticisms of the war or advocated peace. It was a difficult one to answer. Having got the cry well into circulation, and the rumours

as to his honesty passing from one to another,
the Government issued a warrant for his arrest,
not as a dangerous agitator or revolutionary,
but as a traitor. At the same time it set out
to behead the Bolshevik organisation by re-
moving its leaders. Lenin, very conscious of
his own innocence, was inclined to face a trial.
His comrades saw the danger of letting their
leader into the hands of the authorities on any
pretext, and forced him into hiding. This was
a bitter pill to swallow. It would look like
running away from the charge. It would take
his hand off the plough just when the furrow
was really worth ploughing. His objections
were overruled and the difficulty met to some
extent by finding a hiding-place in the vicinity
of Petrograd where easy contact was possible.
From there he could direct operations. This
retreat served for a period, but he had to move
further and then still further afield into Finland.

By this time he felt that the time for armed
insurrection was at hand. Another split had
taken place in the Government. Kerensky was
now at the head, with virtual dictatorial powers.
His supremacy was challenged by some of the
army officers who had their regiments at their
back, and they made a military advance on
Petrograd with the intention of setting up a

military dictatorship under Kornilov. Against this menace all the revolutionary elements in the city combined and the adventure was nipped in the bud. The Bolsheviks played their part with the other sections, felt their growing power, and overcame the psychological difficulty that the industrial worker has in taking up arms. The constitution of the Soviets made it possible for their composition to change from week to week, and they were showing more and more in all parts of the country Bolshevik majorities and substantial increases in Bolshevik strength. Elections to the borough and city councils were in progress, and the Party here also was showing that it had the support of large masses of the people. The Baltic Fleet, with its base on Kronstadt, was overwhelmingly in favour of the Bolshevik policy. Lenin felt that the time for action was close at hand, but had some doubts as to the preparedness of his own immediate colleagues. Trotsky describes Lenin's state of mind at this time : ' He saw clearly the moment approaching when everything would be at the knife's edge, and at the same time he was of the opinion, and not without grounds, that the chiefs of the Party did not draw all the necessary conclusions. The deportment of the Central Committee seemed to him too passive and dilatory. Lenin did not feel it yet possible to return openly to the work, because he feared that his imprisonment might strengthen the dilatoriness of the Party leaders, which would inevitably have led to the neglect of the extraordinary revolutionary situation. . . . He demanded that we should at once put a real conspiracy to work, surprise the opponent, snatch the power—and then we would see. . . . He had unbounded faith that the masses would and could complete the revolution, but he had not the same conviction in regard to the Party staff. And he realised more and more clearly that there was not a moment to lose. A revolutionary situation cannot arbitrarily be maintained until the moment that the Party is ready to make use of it.' Lenin kept up a daily pressure on his friends to make up their minds for speedy, definite action, yet, in contact daily with quickly moving events, he still found time to write theoretical works, and a large part of *The State and Revolution*, one of his most important works, was completed during this enforced absence. He defined the necessary conditions for revolution : ' When a revolutionary party has not the support of a majority either among the vanguard of the revolutionary class, or among the rural population, there can be no question of a rising. A rising must not only have this majority, but must have : (1) the incoming revolutionary tide over the whole country ; (2) the complete moral and political bankruptcy of the old régime, for instance, the Coalition Government ; and (3) a deep-seated sense of insecurity among all the irresolute elements.' He believed that all these conditions were satisfied in Russia by the end of September. As evidence of the incoming revolutionary tide he had the amazing fact that the membership of the Bolshevik Party had increased from about 70,000 to 200,000 in the course of two or three months. The voting in Soviets and borough elections showed a steady increase in Bolshevik strength. The failure of the Government to rouse the Army to fight, and its failure to keep the industrial life of the nation going, or to prevent deliberate sabotage by the owners of factories, were all evidences of its demoralisation. These facts were to his mind arguments for an immediate rising. To some of his closest associates they were reasons against any uprising at all. With the tide flowing so strongly in their direction, Zinoviev and Kamenev felt a rising unnecessary. They believed they would, in this state of the public mind, get a majority in the Constituent Assembly. Trotsky put up a different proposal to both sides. He wished to associate the seizure of power with the meeting of the Second Congress of the Soviets. Lenin beat down the oppositions, and persuaded his comrades that an armed rising was necessary, and that the date must be fixed for it and the plans definitely made.

The condition of the people on the eve of the rising is portrayed by the American writer, John Reed, in his book, *Ten Days that Shook the World* : ' Week by week food became scarcer. The daily allowance of bread fell from a pound and a half to a pound, then to three-quarters, half, and a quarter pound. Toward the end there was a week without any bread at all. Sugar one was entitled to at the rate of two pounds a month—if one could get it at all, which was seldom. A bar of chocolate or a pound of tasteless candy cost anywhere from seven to ten roubles—at least half a dollar. There was milk for about half the babies in the city ; most hotels and private houses never saw it for months.' Again, quoting a statement of a soldier delegate of the Eighth Army, he indicates the condition of the Army : ' We are weak, we have only a few men left in each company. They must give us food and boots

and reinforcements or soon there will be left
only empty trenches. Peace or supplies . . .
either let the Government end the war or support the Army.' The Bolshevik propagandists
toured the country, visited the workshops,
attended Soviet meetings, stirred up the people
and urged the necessity of the armed rising.
The Red Guards drilled openly with arms, and
the Petrograd Soviet elected a Military Revolutionary Committee. The Government did
its best to stem the tide. They endeavoured to
move revolutionary regiments out of Petrograd
and to move loyal ones in. They appointed one
of their number Special Commissar to maintain
order in the city. The Petrograd Garrison
passed a resolution declaring its allegiance to
the Soviet. The delegates from all parts of
Russia began to arrive for the All-Russian Soviet
Congress, and proved to be overwhelmingly
Bolshevik in outlook.

The Soviet occupied the Smolny Institute as
its headquarters. Trotsky had been for some
time President of the Petrograd Soviet, and the
place was already beginning to take on the
appearance of a Governmental centre. Every
order or proclamation from the Provisional
Government was met by another from the
Soviet, issuing contrary instructions. Lenin

returned to the outskirts of the city to be at hand.
The day for the rising was fixed for the 7th
November, the day when the All-Russian Congress of Soviets was to open. On the day
previous the Petrograd Soviet was in session.
It sat well on into the morning of the 7th, the
different Socialist factions struggling with each
other for their own particular policy, but with
the Bolsheviks dominating in strength. By the
early hours of the morning the rising was in
progress. Lenin had mapped out in advance
the strategic points to be seized, resolved that
the mistakes of 1905 should not be repeated.
He had arranged the time of the rising :
' November the 6th will be too early. We must
have an all-Russian basis for the rising, and on
the 6th all the delegates to the Congress will
not have arrived. On the other hand November 8th will be too late. By that time the
Congress will be organised, and it is difficult for
a large body of people to take swift, decisive
action. We must act on the 7th, the day the
Congress meets, so that we may say to it,
" Here is the power ! What are you going to
do with it ? " ' Trotsky, who was issuing the
authoritative statements on behalf of the Soviet,
announced : ' We are asked if we intend to
have a rising. I can give a clear answer to

that question. The Petrograd Soviet feels that at last the moment has arrived when the power must fall into the hands of the Soviets. This transfer of government will be accomplished by the All-Russian Congress. Whether an armed demonstration is necessary will depend on those who wish to interfere with the All-Russian Congress.'

Technically the Provisional Government struck the first blow. Soldiers were sent to close down the Bolshevik newspapers. The Soviet soldiers opened them up again, and proceeded to close down the Government newspapers. Action followed speedily. The Revolutionary forces occupied the Government buildings one by one, the Telephone Exchange, the Telegraph Agency, the State Bank, without opposition. As Lord Emmott says in his Report on the events, 'the Provisional Government simply melted away.' Inside twenty-four hours the Soviet felt that it had assumed authority. Resistance was of the feeblest. More words than bullets were fired. The planning, the timing, the agitation of the master mind had all worked to the demoralisation of the opposing forces. Inside a few hours a proclamation was distributed in every corner of the city :

' To the Citizens of Russia !

' The Provisional Government is deposed. The State Power has passed into the hands of the organ of the Petrograd Soviet of Workers' and Soldiers' Deputies, the Military Revolutionary Committee which stands at the head of the Petrograd proletariat and garrison.

' The cause for which the people were fighting : immediate proposal of a democratic peace, abolition of landlord property-rights over the land, labour control over production, creation of a Soviet Government—that cause is securely achieved.

' LONG LIVE THE REVOLUTION OF WORKMEN, SOLDIERS AND PEASANTS ! '

This proclamation might have seemed a little premature in its confident statement of achievement, but the facts were already justifying confidence. Resistance to their authority was already practically non-existent. The principal Ministers of the Provisional Government were in prison, except Kerensky, who had departed hurriedly from the city to try to find military support at the front, but messages were already coming from the Army declaring support for the new power. Within a few more hours the Government was formed with Lenin as President and Trotsky as Foreign Minister. Lenin took command of affairs at once. There had been some consideration as to whether the Government should be exclusively Bolshevik, or should include members of other Socialist parties. Lenin was agreeable to the wider form, but laid down conditions. These were accepted by the Left Social Revolutionaries.

By the evening of the 8th November Lenin was ready to meet the Congress of the Soviets with his Government arranged, his peace policy ready to be announced to the world, and his land decrees definitely formulated. John Reed describes his appearance : ' It was just 8.40 when a thundering wave of cheers announced the entrance of the Presidium, with Lenin, the great Lenin, among them. A short stocky figure with a big head set down on his shoulders, bald and bulging. Little eyes, a snubbish nose, wide generous mouth and heavy chin ; clean shaven now, but already beginning to bristle with the well-known beard of his past and future. Dressed in shabby clothes, his trousers much too long for him. Unimpressive to be the idol of a mob. A strange popular leader—a leader purely by virtue of intellect ; colourless, humourless, uncompromising and detached, without picturesque idiosyncrasies—but with the power of explaining profound ideas in simple terms, of analysing a concrete situation. And combining with shrewdness, the greatest intellectual audacity.' This was the picture presented by the new ruler of Russia as he walked on to the stage at the Smolny Institute on the 8th November 1917, his first appearance before the people of Russia as the man whose brain would control and direct their affairs through the few years of life remaining to him.

Within another twenty-four hours he was a world figure, and the history of the world began to change its direction. Few in Russia, and practically none outside, believed that his power would be of longer duration than that of his immediate predecessors. Many of his immediate supporters and lieutenants showed by their utterances that they themselves did not hope to hold power for many days. He himself had no doubts. History had decreed that it must be. Marx had explained beyond possibility of denial that power must come to the workers, and that power must be used to establish Socialism. These things were inevitable. He was merely the instrument chosen by the forces that compel history to be made, and he, no more than the Czar, could escape his destiny.

XVI

Lenin was not a passive, unconscious instrument of events. On the contrary he was an active, conscious, understanding director of events. His part was not to pass his responsibilities on, either to the Allies or to an electorate. Things had to be done, and done at once. He was the man in whom had been reposed the power to do them, and he intended to do them. He had to establish order, destroy capitalist power, crush out the possibility of counter-revolution, secure peace, give the land to the people and conquer famine. Any one of these, or a part of any one of them, would have been enough to occupy one man for a long period. Lenin tackled the lot as if they were to be completed in the next twenty-four hours, and shouldered in addition one other task, which did not seem to press so immediately, the call for world revolution.

From this date onward his life was lived in a blaze of publicity. From every corner of the world the spot-lights shone on him, and his every action was discussed and rediscussed. Pilgrims, spies, interested observers came to Russia from all over the world to see this new phenomenon. Each returned to his place of origin and gave his own account of what he had seen. Newspaper correspondents sent their reports to their papers, and the editors wrote leading articles. Public opinion was whipped up to develop an antagonism against this revolutionary innovator. There was an abundance of material for the use of the enemy. Lenin broke every precedent in government. He failed to act in keeping with the ethical maxims of Utopian Socialism. He flung to the four winds the recognised methods of democracy. He silenced his critics by force. He shut down newspapers. He suppressed rebellion with an iron hand. He even went so far as to call the members of his government ' Commissars ' instead of Ministers. The right-thinking bourgeois world was horrified. It was true that every one of both the Allied and the Entente countries had done one or other or all these things during the course of the war. Elections had been suspended, critics imprisoned, rebels shot down, news censored and newspapers suppressed. But that was different. These things were essential to the effective prosecution of the war, and the war was for the preservation of civilisation.

With terrific concentration the new Dictator bent to his task and allowed the storm of denunciation to proceed. Every Government in the world hoped that he would fail. Working people in different lands who felt sympathetic chords touched in their own hearts by this uprising of their class in Russia feared that he could not possibly succeed. He had to face a task of greater dimensions and greater complexity than any statesman, ruler or tyrant had ever confronted. He had to spread his power over the biggest land surface comprised in any nation. He had to bend to his will a population of a hundred and fifty million people. He had to improvise a new machinery of legislation and administration. He had to bring the population to make an intellectual break with the traditions of centuries, and to become the conscious builders of a new society. He had to do these things with practically nothing but his own brain, his own will power and a theory. His own Party members were in the main raw recruits to Bolshevism ; the Party had grown in less than six months from a few tens of thousands to half a million ; among the older and most influential members were several who had so absorbed Socialist theory as to be theory-ridden. The mass of the people were definite enough as to what they desired, but they were quite vague as to how they were to realise their desires. They had developed an aptitude for overthrowing governments : they had disposed of four in eight months, and it could very easily have become a habit. A Constituent Assembly was on the point of meeting. It had been elected in conformity with the best democratic models, and it would afford the possibility of another change of government. Lenin dismissed it summarily when it met. His mandate from the people, he believed, was a better and a stronger one than that of the Constituent Assembly. It would only be in the way, and there was work to be done.

Peace had to be obtained speedily. Lenin would have preferred war directed towards revolutionary ends, but the soldiers had voted for peace by refusing to fight, by walking out of the trenches. They should get it. It would be a bad and a humiliating peace, but it would be peace. He despatched his Commissar for Foreign Affairs, Trotsky, to carry through the negotiations. He published to the world the secret treaties which the Czarist Government had entered into with the Allies, disclosing to the peoples of the combatant countries the imperialist aims of their rulers. After an abortive attempt to evade the signing of a treaty imposed by force, Trotsky very unwillingly accepted the peace of Brest Litovsk. A leading Bolshevik tells a story that is good enough to be true of how Trotsky found that in concluding the treaty certain formalities would have to be observed, including the attendance at an evening function where he would be expected to wear the recognised evening garb. Greatly perturbed at the thought of donning the conventional dress of the hated bourgeois, he wired Lenin for instructions. Back came the answer : ' If it will help to bring peace, go in a petticoat.' The German Government exacted its full pound of flesh in the treaty. Lenin, still hoping for the world revolution, consoled himself with the hope that the uprising of the German workers would change all that. Although he did not live to see the world revolution, nor a German Social revolution, he did see the sympathy and support of his people depart from the Kaiser as they had left the Czar. He saw the establishment of a German Republic, but he saw also the defeat of his friend and comrade, Karl

Liebknecht, whose Spartacist uprising attempted to take the German people along the road that Russia had travelled. His successors to-day see Germany still struggling to solve the contradictions of their capitalist system, and its Government still struggling to fulfil the humiliating terms of the peace treaty of Versailles.

His peace negotiations abroad were not accompanied by conditions of ease at home. The dismissed Duma members, the Constituent Assembly which had been flouted, the deposed Prime Minister, Kerensky, were all forces working to disturb the peace. The black-coated workers in the public offices, the Civil Service in general, took up an attitude of hostility. They refused to work, or where they worked, worked mischief. Ruthlessly he cleared them out and put in loyal workers to perform their duties. He laid down the principle, ' no work, no food.' The bankers refused to open their safes or to give up the keys. They were opened by dynamite. A more serious menace was the refusal of the telegraphists and the railwaymen to carry on their work, for this made communication with the rest of Russia slow at a time when speed was essential. The wireless station still worked, and some aeroplanes were available. These were worked overtime.

The deposed politicians formed a committee of all the anti-Bolshevik elements, entitled ' the Committee for the Salvation of Country and Revolution,' and set out to develop an organisation in the city and the country. The General Officer commanding the forces refused orders, and a young Bolshevik, Krylenko, was appointed in his place. He was promoted from the lowest military rank to the highest in five minutes. It was a gesture of supreme contempt for the servants of the old order. Kerensky, after many rebuffs from the soldiers, managed to collect some forces behind him and began to march on Petrograd. As they got near to the city the revolution in the air began to get into the blood of his Cossacks. After one engagement between them and the Soviet forces they had had enough. They turned against Kerensky, who took refuge in flight. His defeat and departure was a crushing blow to the anti-Bolshevik movement. Revolution spread over the country. City after city, town after town followed Petrograd's example. In some there were days of severe fighting ; in others power passed to the people with scarcely the striking of a blow. In the rural areas the peasants did their best to see that their special interest, the getting of land, should not go unsatisfied.

The leader sat in his headquarters at the Smolny Institute, working, eating, sleeping there. He persuaded, he coaxed, he threatened, he bullied and terrorised. He turned his Socialist agitator friends into a Government, to act as a Government and think as a Government. He turned rioters and pillagers into a disciplined army of Ironsides. He crushed his opponents and critics. In a Report by a British Government Commission under the Chairmanship of Lord Emmott on the political and economic situation in Russia, which was issued in 1921, it was stated that the Bolsheviks ruled without resort to terror for the first few months, but later, when crime and brigandage were rampant, the All-Russian Extraordinary Commission was appointed to restore order. Its activities were directed against sabotage, counter-revolution, speculation, crime in Government service, brigandage, peasant revolts and desertion. Its methods were short and sharp, and large numbers of people undoubtedly suffered death and imprisonment. The execution of the Czar and his family, which had taken place at a somewhat earlier date, was not on the initiative of the Central Government ; and reports agree that Lenin was opposed to the execution of the Czar on grounds of international policy, and of his family on grounds of humanity. The Ural Committee of the Bolsheviks, who had responsibility for the Czar's detention, forced the hands of the Central Government, and the executions took place. General Graves, who commanded the United States Army supporting the Koltchak counter-revolutionary adventure in Siberia in 1919, states in his book, *America's Siberian Adventure* : 'There were horrible murders committed, but they were not committed by the Bolsheviks, as the world believes. I am well on the side of safety when I say that the anti-Bolsheviks killed one hundred people in Eastern Siberia to every one killed by the Bolsheviks.' There may be speculation among pacifists and humanitarians as to whether Lenin could have established peace and order throughout the great Russian territory without resort to methods of violence, and as to whether a Socialist Government is entitled to have recourse to the method of force, which has been and is the ultimate instrument of all capitalist Governments ; but those who support and approve the method of force cannot deny that in the hands of the Bolshevik rulers of Russia, it did prove efficacious in restoring order and in repelling foreign aggression. In the spring of 1918 Lenin had almost created a governmental instrument capable of performing its work. Twelve months' concentration on the problems of peace construction would have worked wonders, and saved untold misery and death. Lenin earnestly longed for it. He wanted the peasant to sow his crops, the miner to dig coal, the builder to erect houses without interruption. His wish was not to be granted.

XVII

Neither the Allies nor the Entente Powers were satisfied with the way Russia was acting. The war was still in progress ; bitterness between the two sides was at its keenest. Neither side was managing its affairs very well. Grave discontent was being manifested by their civilian populations. No obvious progress was being made in the hostilities ; every day thousands of men were killed or maimed in the mud and barbed wire. Death rained from the sky, shot up from the sea and spread over the earth's surface. The two antagonists had, however, one common ground ; they believed they could manage Russian affairs infinitely better than Russia was managing them herself. They aided and abetted, financed and armed the various Russian adventurers, military and naval, who came forward to offer themselves as Russia's saviours.

Russia had to expend over two years in repelling the attacks of counter-revolutionary forces led by Admiral Koltchak, General Deni-

kin and General Wrangel. Each one of these
counter-revolutionary movements was made
separately and independently of each other,
and operated in different parts of the country.
The crushing of them meant a tremendous
drain on the reduced resources of the nation,
and a tremendous strain on the man who sat
at the centre of power.

In August 1918 he had been shot by the
Social Revolutionary, Dora Kaplan. He took
a bare three weeks in the country to recover
from his wound, and returned to his desk
again. His danger aroused the spirit of the
people as never before. His personal prestige
rose to a high point, and the threats against
the Government by the counter-revolutionists
produced a national consciousness ready to
offer resistance to aggression. Poland, under
Marshal Pilsudski, added its power to the
other attempts against the Russian Government, and the Russian effort against Poland
passed from pure defence into definite attack.
This represented a great change in the morale
of the people since the days of 1917 when the
soldiers walked out of the trenches. The change
was not due to any substantial improvement
in the material conditions of the people, for,
blockaded on all sides as they were, and unable

to proceed effectively with home production, their material conditions were very bad. It was a marvellous manifestation of faith-healing, faith in a cause, faith in the man who personified that cause.

At last all attacks were repulsed ; peace came to the land, and Lenin could turn his attention to economic reconstruction. It was high time. Evidences of discontent were showing in one or two places, among the peasants and the Kronstadt sailors. They were easily put down ; but Lenin believed that they were symptoms of genuine grievance and set himself to remedy the grievance without delay. He decreed that the War Communism, the strong central control of production and distribution which had been imposed, should be relaxed ! The peasant should not be liable to the appropriation of his whole crop or whatever proportion of it the local Soviet officials felt necessary. His proportion should be fixed and definite, and with the residue he should be permitted to trade as he pleased. Private traders who had been driven out of business were allowed to resume trading. Certain concessions for industrial production were granted to foreign capitalists. These changes, termed the New Economic Policy, were a *volte-*

face with a vengeance. It took all Lenin's power to persuade his Bolshevik comrades that it was not a retreat from Socialism that would end in rout. He had to show them that they were strong enough in their control of the essentials of economic power to prevent the policy from going beyond the point where it was useful in speedily improving the standards of life of the people. The peasants must be able to feel that the new order meant something of value to them, different from Czarist landlord days. Lenin had appreciated this fact from the beginning of his period of power, but he avoided the battle with the Party that he knew would be necessary to secure acceptance of his view while his chief preoccupations were elsewhere. In the spring of 1921 the new policy was accepted and the Government commenced to put it into operation. Very soon a class of prosperous traders sprang into being, known as the Nepmen, who revived small-scale capitalism at great profit to themselves. But 1921 was still a bad year for Russia. Famine and disease swept the land in acute form, and only a tremendous capacity to endure carried the nation through.

In 1922 Lenin began to feel that his overwrought frame was beginning to rebel. His night-and-day concentration on his work had exhausted the elasticity of his arteries, and they responded less readily to the demands of his brain. He was now fifty-two years of age, and naturally expected a fair span of life to follow. In May his body struck work. He had crushed many mutineers in the previous four years. He had fought anarchy and famine. Now he faced defeat from this new enemy within himself that threatened to destroy him. He gained a temporary victory. After a few months' rest in the country he returned to the post of duty, but in March 1923 another stroke laid him low. Again he fought hard against the inevitable, made some progress, but fell back beaten on the 21st January 1924.

So ended a life that had lasted only fifty-four years : thirty-four years of manhood, the large proportion of which had been spent in prison, exile in Siberia, or in forced emigration outside the borders of Russia. He had had only five years of free activity in Russia before illness struck him and weakened his powers. In that short period he had controlled and directed a Revolution vaster than anything known in history. He had taken his nation out of the European war. He had quelled civil war within her borders. He had fought famine and pestilence. He had developed an economic machine to supply the nation's material needs. He had established a machine of government on an entirely new model deriving its motive power solely from the working class.

When the news of his death spread throughout the world the wise politicians prophesied that the structure he had created would speedily fall to pieces now that the master hand was withdrawn. Eight years have elapsed since his death, and no sign of collapse has been apparent in the Union of Soviet Socialist Republics of Russia. On the contrary, under the central direction of his successor Stalin and his fellow Commissars, Russia has maintained eight years of peace and steady industrial and agricultural progress. Her rivals have waited impatiently for the day when the crash would come, and have persistently and enthusiastically prophesied its coming. Up till now Russia has failed to fulfil their prophecies, and every year has established the Soviet form of government and Socialist ways of life as being the natural and customary state of affairs. Men and women of thirty years of age now were boys and girls of fifteen when the Revolution took place. To them a Soviet Socialist Republic is as natural a form of government as is a limited monarchy to the population of Great Britain. The conservative element in human nature, which always resents and resists change, is on the side of the continuation of the present order in Russia, while the vitalising forces that are necessary for progress draw their energy from the knowledge of a task unfinished, and from the principles which Lenin taught.

The Scottish poet, Robert Burns, in one of his despondent moods arising from a contemplation of the wastage and futility of much of human effort, uttered the words :

> ' The best laid schemes of mice and men
> Gang aft agley,
> And leave us nought but grief and pain
> For promised joy.'

Human experience both of men and of nations supports the truth expressed by the poet. It is true that much human endeavour goes adrift and fails to attain the desired object. It is a good thing for human sanity that while this often happens it does not always happen ; but there are no recorded instances of any scheme on so vast a scale worked out in the mind of one man coming so near to complete achievement as the scheme worked out in the mind of Lenin.

We are still too near to him in time, too close to the happenings incidental to his work, too much under the influence of partisan anti-pathies or sympathies to venture final assess-ments. It is not yet possible to say that Russia has in practice realised the Utopian state of plenty, of liberty and of happiness, nor is it possible to say that other countries may not reach a better state in speedier and less harsh ways. It is possible to say that this man, quiet, unassuming, unimposing, set himself a task of immense size when still a boy, and stuck to it tenaciously to the end of his life. He gave up every joy and reward that men normally seek, and bent his whole being to his self-imposed task. He read history and drew conclusions from it. History did not fail him. The con-clusions that he drew were proved by events to be true conclusions for Russia and for him. There were periods in his life when he could draw no inspiration save from his own inner resources. At critical periods he had to stand alone, his friends aloof. Few of the men who started on the road with him finished the course by his side. He set too hot a pace. He de-manded more sacrifice than most men were ready to give.

To Russia he left a social structure capable

of development to unlimited extent. To the
rest of the world he left a serious problem which
mankind must speedily solve. Can humanity
progress to higher social forms without collapse
of existing forms, entailing widespread suffering ? Can man by force of intelligence go forward to better things, or must he proceed by
way of struggle, violence and brute force?
History is on the side of Lenin's view. At every
big change in social structure there has been an
open clash of opposing forces. He himself was
a personification of brain force, the force of the
idea defeating immeasurably superior force of
arms. The German military might, the military power of France and Britain placed behind
the insurgents in Russia, were beaten more by
the power of his mind and his idea than by the
military organisation that he could bring to
bear against them. Yet he among all his
associates proclaimed most definitely the absolute necessity of physical force as an unavoid-
able incident in the creation of a new social
order.

One looks back through history in vain to
find some one with whom comparison is possible. In the story of religious struggles there
are instances of greater devotion and sacrifice
for a cause. In the stories of war there are

greater generals. In political life there have
been more subtle statesmen. But nowhere is to
be found in any single man the peculiar combination of devotion, courage, wisdom, skill
and human understanding except in the man
Lenin, who will live in history under the name
he chose when his work was carried on in
underground cellars, when he was an outcast
in the land of which he was to become the un-
challenged ruler.

NB Following 1939-46 World War the
closing of Russian minds under Stalin
led to a fantastic image of the world
and a leadership with a near fatal
vision of the west as a nuclear
agressor (oleg. Gordievsky)

Under Gorbachev Peristroika and
Glasnost led to freedom from Communism
for the Eastern states of Europe 1990
and more democratic structures in
USSR with a 5 yr presidency with greater
powers for the elected president than in
any other country in the world, though
the economic conditions were also teetering
173
on the edge of bankruptcy.

*This book is a production of
Heron Books, London*

*This book was printed in England
and bound by Hazell Watson & Viney Ltd,
Aylesbury, Bucks*